D0908838

RAGING BULL

RAGING BULL

The Autobiography of the England Rugby Legend

PHIL VICKERY

WITH ALISON KERVIN

HarperSport
An Imprint of HarperCollins*Publishers*

First published in 2010 by
HarperSport
an imprint of HarperCollins*Publishers*
77–85 Fulham Palace Road
Hammersmith, London W6 8JB

www.harpercollins.co.uk

1 3 5 7 9 10 8 6 4 2

All photographs have been supplied by the author, with the exception of:
Alex Livesey/Getty Images: p7 (bottom); Bryn Lennon/Getty Images: p2
(top); David Rogers/Getty Images: p3 (top and bottom), p4 (top, middle
and bottom), p5 (top right), p6 (middle and bottom), p7 (top and middle);
Mark Thompson/Getty Images: p5 (top left); Patrick Kovarik/AFP: p6 (top);
Popperfoto/Getty Images: p2 (bottom); Ross Land/Getty Images: p5
(bottom); Stu Forster/Getty Images: p3 (middle).

Phil Vickery asserts the moral right to be
identified as the author of this work

A catalogue record of this book is
available from the British Library

ISBN 978-0-00-735421-4

Printed and bound in Great Britain by
Clays Ltd, St Ives plc

Mixed Sources
Product group from well-managed
forests and other controlled sources
www.fsc.org Cert no. SW-COC-001806
© 1996 Forest Stewardship Council
FSC

FSC is a non-profit international organisation established to promote the
responsible management of the world's forests. Products carrying the FSC
label are independently certified to assure customers that they come
from forests that are managed to meet the social, economic and
ecological needs of present and future generations.

Find out more about HarperCollins and the environment at
www.harpercollins.co.uk/green

CONTENTS

To Kate, Megan and Harry

INTRODUCTION

I'm the luckiest bugger in the world. Look at me – this daft bloody farmer from Cornwall and I've travelled the world, been on two Lions tours, two World Cup finals (and won one of them), got an MBE and met the Queen.

Met the Queen. Me! Bloody hell. There I was, this chubby herdsman in a smart suit, standing in the Palace, surrounded by corgis, sipping tea and eating sandwiches without crusts. Who'd have thought it? Not any of my school teachers, that's for sure. Not the guys I grew up with or the mates I went to school with. I don't think anyone who knew me when I was younger would have believed for one minute that I'd end up at Buckingham Palace. It's been a hell of a bloody journey, from doing the milking down on the farm in Bude and kicking balls through Mum's kitchen windows to having tea in the Queen's house and meeting the Prime Minister. It's not all been great, I'll admit. I've had some back operations that would make your eyes water just to think of them, but most of it has been amazing.

The reason it's been amazing? It's because of the people I've met. Daft buggers like me who play in the front row, getting their teeth kicked in and their ears bent inside out ... the real men. You make friends quickly when you're cheek to cheek with a bloke. You learn to respect someone when you see them operate at such close quarters and you know about commitment when you're staring into the eyes of Raphael Ibanez, Oz du Randt or some big bloke known as 'The Beast', and preparing to shove your head next to theirs and force yourself forward with every ounce of strength you've got. It's bloody great when you feel the scrum move forward and you know you've got them. One little power struggle won for you, one little fight lost for them. Best feeling in the world, and I bloody love it.

Mind you, it's not so great in the mornings. I wake up some days after playing and everything hurts. Every muscle feels like it's been smashed to pieces and I'm sure I can hear them screaming when I try to move. Getting out of bed feels like the hardest job in the world. There are days when just moving an arm hurts so much I feel as if I've been shot, but even in the worst moments I wouldn't change any of it. Even on the days after my horrendous operations when I was in so much pain I could hardly see straight, I've never regretted a minute of my life as a rugby player.

I've met some great people, been to some great countries and lived a life that most people dream of. I'm very grateful to have been given the opportunity to do this. I am honoured to carry the dreams of millions when I run out in that white England shirt or the red Lions shirt. It's easy to say 'I feel privileged' but I do. I feel as if I'm the luckiest guy ever.

I've had a hell of a career because so much has changed since I started. Things have happened during my time as a rugby player that have been astonishing to witness – like the game turning from amateur to professional as I was starting out at Gloucester. I'm privileged to have experienced both sides of the sport.

One thing that hasn't changed is the commitment it takes to make it to the top. There's a lovely phrase and I use it all the time ... 'If you're going to fail, die trying.' That's my motto. I believe you should fall at the last; don't cross the line coming second. *Go for it.* I know it's easy to say, and it isn't about rugby or playing for England. To me, it says that, whatever you do in life, give it everything. Fight every problem to the death and throw your weight behind everything that means anything to you. Most of all, have fun doing it.

That philosophy worked for a tubby farmer from Cornwall who got to meet the Queen ...

CHAPTER ONE:

THE BEST PLACE ON EARTH

Cornwall ... I bloody love it. It's a great place, isolated from everywhere and full of the friendliest people in the world. It's more like a village than a county – packed full of daft types who treat each other like one big family. I loved growing up there and hearing about its great history – all the myths and legends from times gone by, the stories about wrecked ships mysteriously disappearing, and tales of strange happenings that no one could explain or seemed to know where they'd come from. There's something about the scenery down in Cornwall and the beauty of the place that inspires writers, poets and musicians and gets people telling tales. There were always famous people moving into the area when I was young, aiming to find creativity on the wide, golden sands, amongst the big cliffs and in the beautiful countryside. I thought I lived in the most special place on earth.

I'm from North Cornwall, where the Atlantic winds come bursting in off the sea. I love the ruggedness of it all. It can be very bleak at times, very dark and moody, but very beautiful at other times. I love the fact that things don't change constantly as they do in other parts of the country. Things stay the same and the people stay the same. It's the place where I grew up, went to school and lived for the first nineteen years of my life – running around on Duckpool beach, diving into the sea and body boarding on the huge waves. Taking my bloody life in my hands as I surfed close to the cliffs, and loving it as the eight-foot swells threw me off my body board. We'd go fishing in the rock pools with Dad and Granddad and mess around on beaches that were so hard to get to from the cliffs that we had to ease one another down on these tatty old ropes we'd found, none of us worrying about how dangerous the whole thing was, or wondering for a second how we were going to get back up again.

When I think back, I can't believe that we were allowed to spend so much time on the beach on our own, but it was a great place to grow up, close to the sea and close to nature. I tell my kids, Megan and Harrison, the stories of when I was a little boy, and it sounds so idyllic. There was something so lovely and adventurous about the freedom we had – life in the fresh air, enjoying long days and warm nights outside.

I'm proud of being a Cornishman ... it's in my blood. So it's slightly odd that one of the first things I have to tell you about myself is that I was born in Devon! Before you think that makes me any less Cornish, I'd better explain. I was born in Barnstaple, in Devon, because my family is from Bude which is a great little seaside town in North Cornwall, and the nearest hospital was just over the county line in Devon. But besides that, I am Cornish through and through.

I was born into a family of big, bulky dairy farmers, with Mum and Dad working on Killock, a 350-acre farm just outside Bude. The farm had originally belonged to my grandparents. Both sets of grandparents are farmers, so dairy farming really is in my blood, and there's no doubt that farming is what I'd have ended up doing if rugby hadn't come along and cocked everything up!

My grandma and grandpa Vickery originally started off life in a place called Bagbury Farm, not far from us in Bude. Then they bought Killock Farm and split the cows between the two farms, making successes of both of them. I do look back and think: Bloody hell, how did they do that? Farming's a difficult business to make a success of with just one farm to look after, but managing to create two farms out of one like that takes some doing. They did it so that my dad, Barry, could be given Killock when he married my mum, Elaine, and his sister, my aunty Carol, could farm Bagbury.

So I lived on Killock Farm with Mum, Dad, my grandparents and my brother Mark who was two years old when I was born. I was surrounded by animals, milking machines and tractors from an early age. It's all I ever knew as a kid. It was a perfect place for an adventurous child to live, and you'll be unsurprised to hear that I was a bloody adventurous child, always exploring, climbing, clambering over everything and generally getting up to mischief on the farm with Mark. I can see now, looking back at the way we were back then, that we must have been a hell of a handful for poor Mum; I don't know how she coped with us rampaging around the place, doing more damage than if a couple of rhinos had been let loose on the farm. She probably spent as long clearing up after us as she did clearing up after the animals.

Mum never had an easy time of it with me because I started causing problems straight away – from the moment I came into the world at Barnstaple Hospital on 14 March 1976, weighing a sprightly 7lb 13½oz. I was heavier than my brother Mark who'd come before me, and heavier than Helen who came along later, but not the super heavyweight you might expect if you look at the size of me now. I was rushed into an incubator straight after I was born having turned a rather unattractive blue colour (the next time I turned that colour was after one of John Mitchell's training sessions, but we'll come onto those later). The doctors were worried about whether I was getting enough oxygen into my body, so decided to keep an eye on me. It meant Mum had to stay in hospital with me for an extra two days before she could take me home.

I'm sure that when Mum eventually got me back to the farm, and realised just what an active and lively child I was going to become, she might have wished I was still in that incubator! She says I was a real handful from the minute she got me back, and with a large dairy farm full of machinery, animals and wide open spaces to mess about in, I had plenty to play with. I didn't waste any time causing mischief and there are all sorts of stories about me gently petting the animals and half killing them. I'm sure they're not true ... especially not the tales about me squashing the little ducklings half to death. Not me, surely.

I was such a bundle of non-stop energy, even when I was tiny, that Mum decided the only way to cope and keep me relatively safe was to shove me into a wooden playpen and tie it to the kitchen table while she was doing chores around the house. (I'm sure that would be illegal now!) If she didn't do that, she said I'd push the pen all around the kitchen until I found something interesting (i.e. breakable) to play with. When she was out on the farm doing jobs, she couldn't leave me for a minute either, so she put me in the hay rack where I couldn't cause much trouble and she could get on with things without worrying where the next big crash was going to come from.

As we grew up and learnt to toddle around the farm, the smacks, bangs, smashes and collisions that Mark and I got into grew too. Mum remembers me coming in one day with a huge gash on my arm after playing outside all day. I wasn't bothered about it at all, in fact I hadn't noticed, but she was so concerned that she rushed me off to hospital to get it checked out. She's still amazed today that I didn't realise there was blood dripping from my arm. All I wanted to do was to keep playing. I guess, looking back, I was always a prop forward in the making.

In this idyllic childhood there was always so much going on in and around the farm. It was all outdoors in the fresh air and I was always surrounded by family. My sister Helen was born three years after me, which didn't please me a lot, apparently. Mum says she can remember coming home from hospital and announcing that we had a new sister and Mark and I looked at one another and frowned in disappointment. We didn't really see the point in having a sister. What were sisters for? They weren't interested in climbing things and causing the mayhem that Mark and I enjoyed, so the two of us pretty much carried on as we had done and tried to forget about the small female who had just joined the family.

I think I spent most of my childhood completely covered in mud. I remember sitting in the sink absolutely filthy after a morning outside, and being cleaned from head to toe by my grandma (with a big lump of old-fashioned soap and some sort of scrubbing brush – I imagine that's the only way they could get the mud off me). When I was clean, I was dressed and then sent back out into the fields where I'd get muddy all over again.

One side of the farm house was rented out when I was growing up, and we lived in the other half. We weren't supposed to mess about around the rented half of the farm. I can remember the sound of Mum's voice as she told us to keep away from there but of course that didn't stop us at all, and if there were no adults there, that's where Mark and I could be found – with a football.

Belting footballs through the windows of the house was something that Mark and I did quite frequently. We'd be kicking the ball backwards and forwards to one another, and trying to kick it over the house and round the house, but our kicking skills weren't as refined as we'd hoped, so invariably there would come a point where we kicked the ball *through* the house (via the window). There'd be that horrible sound of smashing glass and a split second of silence in which we looked at one another and realised that we were in big trouble.

We knew that Mum would go nuts when she found out we'd smashed a window, so every time the ball crashed through the glass we'd stand there and look at one another for a minute, then run away from the scene as fast as we could. It makes me laugh to look back now. What did we think would happen? Surely we must have realised that Mum would take one look at the broken window, the football lying on the kitchen floor and the glass all around and realise straight away what had happened. It seems odd that we ran away, thinking that we might just get away with it. We never did.

My first experiences of life off the farm were at a local nursery school, where I went a couple of mornings a week, then it was on to Kilkhampton Primary School for slightly more serious schooling and, more importantly, the chance to get involved in lots of different sports like cricket, foot-ball and rounders for the first time. I'm not from a sporty family, and my parents aren't sporty at all (the only sports event I ever saw my dad compete in was a young farmers' tug-of-war one year), but when I got to school I became very interested in all sports, and I wanted to get involved with everything that the school had to offer. Mark was the same as me and we would play all sorts of sports together.

We even enjoyed darts – that was fun. We would prac-tise at home with a makeshift set-up. We'd fix up a dart-board on the chair leaning against the kitchen table, and throw arrows at it, practising our technique as we competed against one another to get the better score. Again, this was a case of our skills not being quite as good as we envisaged, and we'd miss the dartboard frequently, and leave loads of little holes all over Mum's best chairs and table. Once again, we'd run away from the scene and hope she'd not notice. She always did.

As we got older our love for darts continued to blossom, but we moved ourselves from hurling arrows at Mum's best furniture to throwing them at the dartboard in the pub where we could do a lot less damage, get into a hell of a lot less trouble and drink pints. We even went on to play in the local leagues against other pubs in the area; we all took it very seriously.

Back on the farm, we spent a lot of time razzing around the place on tractors and when I look back now I can see that I was a bit of a liability. I just seemed to crash the bloody thing all the time (I think you'll notice there's a theme developing here ... I did have a habit of breaking a lot of things). There were these small walls all around the farm, and I have to tell you that small walls and big tractors don't make a very happy combination. You'd drive along in the tractor and just not see them. The trouble is, even though they were only small and didn't look like they'd do any damage at all, if you hit them with the tractor, you would end up ripping the tyres off, which cost hundreds of pounds to repair. Dad would go mad.

As we got older, so the trouble we got into became bigger. One particular story I remember was of my brother racing around the farm on a quad bike. He and I were out doing the fencing (repairing holes in the hedges to stop the sheep breaking out). We had just finished the job and were heading for home when we realised we'd left something right at the bottom of the field. It was a really foggy day, so Mark went off on his quad bike to get it, and I waited on the tractor for him to come back. He disappeared into the foggy mist, out of sight, while I waited patiently. The next thing I knew, there was the most almighty crash – he'd driven straight into an electric pole and smashed the front of the quad bike. Luckily he went flying off to one side and was uninjured. To be honest, though, his injuries were the least of my concern. I saw the front of the quad bike and the way it was all smashed in, and all I could think was, 'What the hell are we going to tell Dad?'

Again, Dad was really unhappy. But not quite as cross as he was when it came to tractor mirrors and windows. Christ, he'd get pissed off with us. Not that I can blame him because we did smash a lot of them. The windows at the back of the tractor were a particular problem because they opened outwards, so I'd shove them open on a pleasant day, and immediately forget that I'd done it. I would reverse the tractor up to something, forgetting that the windows added another foot onto the length of the tractor behind me, and hear a loud crash and the smash of glass. Shit! This happened so many times that Dad eventually refused to replace the back windows. On freezing cold winter days we would always regret our recklessness, as we sat there wrapped up in coats, hats and gloves, freezing bloody cold.

Although Mark and I played around a lot, we also helped out on the farm from quite a young age. Certainly by the time I was four I was doing chores regularly. The rule in farming tends to be that as soon as you're strong enough to do something, you're old enough. I remember having some funny little jobs, like filling gaps in the hedge to stop the cattle running through. I guess it's like an apprenticeship. You master all the tasks that your father does by watching, helping him, then doing them yourself.

That's why farms are passed down through the generations, because of all the small things you learn growing
up. As soon as I was able to lift bales of hay, I would be
lifting them, and as soon as I could milk the cows, I did
that. It was a gradual thing, until I could do everything on
the farm for myself.

I loved farming but it's a hard, hard job because it never
stops. One thing that people tend to forget about farming is that there's no such thing as a weekend. The cows
need milking every day, and that includes Christmas Day,
birthdays, and every weekend, morning and night. In fact,
in order to minimise the workload on Christmas Day we
used to double up on everything so that we wouldn't
have to work like mad on 25 December itself. It meant
that the period leading up to Christmas would be very
hard work, ensuring there'd be enough hay, straw and
feed to allow us to get through. Christmas parties were a
thing that other people did.

Without doubt, the most difficult thing to happen
when I was young was Mum and Dad splitting up. I was
around eight years old at the time, and though I was very
young I remember it all clearly. There had been lots of
rows in the house and lots of tension in the air leading up
to their decision, so looking back I can see it was the best
thing, but at the time I didn't understand at all. I'd hear
Dad shouting and Mum crying but you still never imagine
that your parents will split. It's a terrible shock when it
actually happens.

When they separated, Mum and Dad decided that
Mum should move out, leaving Dad, my grandparents,
me, Mark and Helen on the farm. Once Mum had settled

somewhere new, we went to live with her. Mum and Dad tried a couple of times to get back together, but it didn't work out, so we moved back and forth between Mum's new house and the farm.

I found the whole divorce thing hard. I was old enough to know that things were changing and life was about to become more confusing than ever. I can remember over-hearing my parents saying, 'He's too young to under-stand,' when talking about the divorce. That's something that still frustrates me to this day. Of course I wasn't too young. I was aware that all these things were happening around me, but no one would explain them to me.

I'm not blaming anyone. I think Mum and Dad didn't want to burden me with all the details because they thought I was too young, and that I would adjust better if I wasn't weighed down with too much information. In reality, though, I think it would have been better if I had been talked to properly and told what was happening. I think you have to know all the details in order to be able to deal with the things that happen to you, even when you're very young.

It was difficult when the split first happened, but we soon settled into a routine. There is no doubt that my parents splitting up had an effect on me. If you come from a broken home I think it makes you tougher and less trusting of people. It makes you harder, and I know I've carried that with me. It's not a bad thing, necessarily; it's just a fact of life.

When I wasn't at the farm, I was at school. One of the clearest memories I have of my junior school is that it was much bigger than infants school; in fact I remember it being huge. I was daunted by the enormous size of it, and thought I'd never be able to find my way around. I recently went back there for the school's centenary and it made me laugh how tiny everything was. The class-rooms were so small and the chairs so little, but when I was young it seemed like a really big place. I was never very confident when it came to school work, and though I tried my hardest when I was younger (the same can't be said of me when I was older) I did find it tough going. I guess I never really saw the point of school. I never imag-ined myself doing anything but farming at the end of it all, so what was the point? It always seemed to me that being on the farm was the best place in the world to be.

When I was 11 I moved to Budehaven School where I continued my dislike of school work. We were living back at the farm with Dad at this stage, and a bus would come to collect us every morning at the end of the lane to take us there. I used to get up at around 8.15 a.m. and didn't have to help too much on the farm before school, but there were always little things to do. My greatest memory of that time is the battle to get someone to drive me and my brother to the end of the lane so we could get the bus. The lane was around half a mile long and on cold winter days, or rainy days, we would be eager to persuade someone to give us a lift. Obviously, everyone else in the family was knee deep in chores at that time in the morn-ing, and they were reluctant to break away from them to take us to the bus stop.

When I got to school, I spent most of the days looking out of the window during lessons. I loved the friends I'd made, and if it hadn't been for them I doubt my parents would have got me anywhere near the school at all. I'm not saying it was all bad. I remember that I enjoyed subjects like history, but I was never very good at spelling so my confidence was dented from the start. It's hard if you have no confidence in yourself. I'd sit at the back of the room and not focus on what was happening in front of me. I guess I just wasn't ever a great scholar (and that's an understatement). There was nothing wrong with the school, or the teachers, it was just me. At that age I simply wasn't interested. It was only PE lessons and break-time that held any interest for me at all.

Thanks to my PE teacher, school didn't turn out to be a complete waste of time.

CHAPTER TWO:

BUDE HEAVEN

My PE teacher at Budehaven School was a great man called Mr Opie. I should tell you a few things about this guy because it was thanks to him that my rugby career started in the first place. He was everything a kid could ever want in a school teacher – encouraging, enthusiastic and passionate about sport. He was very keen that we should try out all sports and not just decide that we were footballers or rugby players and stick to that. I am really pleased about this now, because although I've made rugby my life, I'm also a huge cricket fan (if not a great player) and have a rounded view of sport.

There's no question, though, that Mr Opie had a particular fondness for rugby. I think he could see that with a little guidance and encouragement I had the makings of a decent player, and he was very keen for me to go down to Bude, the local rugby club, to have a go at playing the game in a more competitive environment. One of the saddest things for me was that Mr Opie died before I was capped for England, so he never saw just how far I went in my rugby career. I've raised a glass to the guy on many occasions in thanks for everything he did for me and for other kids in the school.

When Mr Opie suggested going down to Bude to play the game, I admit that I was very open to the idea. My brother Mark had gone down there a few years before me, and he seemed to be having a great time. I didn't hear much about the rugby he was playing but had heard all about the good friends, brilliant away trips and the thrill of matches. So when I was 13 I made my first visit to the club, and I was hooked from the start. I loved it.

There were no mini or youth sides back then, so by the time I was 15 I was playing in the Colts. I don't think they would allow you to do that now because there are sides for all age groups up to Colts level, but back then I guess the philosophy was the same as Dad's on the farm – if you're big enough and tough enough, you're old enough. Anyway, it suited me. At Bude they upheld the great traditions of the sport, and I'm glad, looking back, that I began my rugby career there.

Many of those traditions, of course, involved embarrassing the players as much as humanly possible. There was a game played there where you had to run round the field naked and the last one back got chucked in the river. The worst one, though, was the naked run through Bude ... if you did something wrong on the minibus you'd be chucked out and have to run home without any clothes on. It's great, isn't it? Wherever you play rugby in the world they're always up to things like that. Long may it continue!

I loved rugby down at Bude because it was such a huge escape from normal life. You could dive around tackling people legally, you were completely let loose and could do whatever you wanted to stop people with the ball. I am reasonably quiet – always have been – and I don't tend to get angry or raise my voice, no matter what happens, but on the rugby pitch I got a new lease of life. It was an opportunity to be completely free and to make things happen – no shackles or ties, you weren't told which bits of the field you could stand in, and which bits you couldn't.

I played alongside Mark in the Bude Colts side, which was great. Mum and my grandparents would come down to watch us. Mark was hooker and I was prop, and we made a formidable front row. I imagined that we'd always play together but that wasn't to be because I moved on from Bude after just a couple of years, and Mark stayed there. I guess Mark lacked the discipline to dramatically improve his game where rugby was concerned. That's not a criticism at all, I just think that he probably didn't want it enough to work that much harder to improve, and combined with injuries it never worked out for him. It's funny what makes a top-class player, and what the differences are between those who get to the top and those who don't. Temperament might have something to do with it. For reasons that are diffi-cult to explain, I was the one willing to work at my game and determined to improve while Mark was less both-ered. People say I'm a mixture of my Mum and Dad, while Mark is more like Dad. I think I'm most like my Grandfather Vickery – a gentle giant. I'm a traditional middle child. Perhaps it's something to do with that, or perhaps I had more to prove because I'd been more deeply affected by Mum and Dad's divorce. Who knows? There's a thin line between those who make it and those who don't and I think it's very hard to say why some players make it and some very good, talented players don't.

Once I started to get into rugby at Bude, I paid much more attention to the sport generally, and began watching it on television. I remember the excitement at hearing the BBC's *Grandstand* music and seeing the images of Will Carling, Wade Dooley, Mike Teague and Jon Webb – these hero figures who were just brilliant at their sport. It never crossed my mind that I would get there and be playing with them one day; it never occurred to me that I should be trying to get there, or would want to get there. These were just alien beings I loved to watch on television whose rugby skills were so much better than mine. I never counted myself as being like them in any way. I just played my best at Bude, then went home and worked on the farm. The guys on the television were something else – they were truly gifted.

In 1991 I went to Twickenham to watch Cornwall play against Yorkshire in the county final. It was a big occasion for us and we had a coach-load going up from Bude Rugby Club for the day, all of us dressed in the black and yellow colours of Cornwall. The county game is still extremely strong in the West Country and we made a real day of it, stopping to play Cobham Rugby Club en route. I loved being at Twickenham that day and chatting away to the Yorkshire supporters, as kids from opposite ends of the country stood together supporting the best in county rugby.

There was a whole crowd of us there from Bude, mostly from the club, but other non-rugby supporters had come from the town just to support the county and enjoy a bloody good day out. I had lots of friends in the local village; it was such a small place that everyone knew everyone else. Some of the guys in the village were farmers like me, some were in the building trade, most had physical jobs of some sort and loved their rugby. We all ran onto the pitch afterwards to pull up the turf. Everyone wanted a memory of Cornwall's victory. I remember going back home and me and Mark arriving back in Bude, and sitting down by the river after the coach had dropped us off. A police car came along and asked us whether we were OK. 'We're fine, we've just been to Twickenham for the match,' we explained. The policeman told us to get in, and he gave us a lift home. Bude was that kind of place. There was little trouble and little to worry about.

While things were going extremely well at the rugby club, I continued playing at school too. I played U15 Cornwall trials as well as working my way through the age group levels for England Schools. One of the clearest memories I have is of playing for the England U16s at Pontypridd. Christ, it was amazing. It was the first time I'd sung the national anthem on the pitch, and that was the biggest thrill for me. I thought I'd burst with pride. There we were in the valleys, in the heart of Wales where they love their rugby and passionately support their team, belting out the national anthem while dressed in England colours. It made me feel great. That to me is what playing for your country is all about – the pride you feel and the commitment to the players alongside you. Bloody awesome. There's nothing like it. I loved that first match because there were no expectations. It was just me in this great team, trying to play the best I could. When you become more successful, people's expectations of you rise. People expect you to do well, and pressure comes from trying to live up to those expectations. But that day in Pontypridd, everything was new, fresh and exciting.

When I came back from the game, I found I had a new nickname, after the local newspaper called me 'The Dude from Bude'. Like all these things, it stuck for a while, which was a bit embarrassing, but because I didn't rise to it when people called me it, they soon stopped bothering!

Being 15 and being spotted by senior coaches in the England set-up was extremely exciting, but for me it was all about enjoyment of the game rather than ambition or achievement. Rugby was fun. Sure, playing in an England shirt was fantastic but one of my philosophies in life is not to take things too seriously – you have to have fun or you don't do it. People started asking me where I saw my future and what my career progression in rugby was likely to be, and I just looked at them like they were nuts. I played rugby because I enjoyed it and I never wanted to lose sight of that.

I started rugby because I enjoyed the friendships and the fun, and that's why I stuck with it. When I became a professional rugby player, and I had to take it more seriously than I did when I was a teenager in Cornwall, I put the necessary hours in to training and fitness work, but it didn't change the fact that the most important thing was to have fun.

Having said that, while I was focused on having fun, the whole thing can't have been that enjoyable for Mum! When I look back, she must have driven me miles and miles and miles as I travelled to selection days, training sessions and matches. How did she do it? I don't know how she managed to combine working with bringing up my brother and sister, and driving me around the country. The trial system involves a lot of travelling wherever you are, but if you're based in Cornwall it seems to involve more than most. I can remember going to all sorts of trials, first within the county, with East Cornwall playing against West Cornwall, then I got into the Cornwall side as a result. We then ended up playing county games against sides like Devon and Avon & Somerset. I think there was one against Gloucestershire as well, so there was a bit of travelling involved.

The better I got, and the more advanced, the further away from Cornwall I had to travel. Once I'd excelled in the county games, I was asked to attend trials for the south-west. Now the south-west is a bloody big place so the journeys were further and taking longer. Mum enlisted the help of Mrs Risden, our next-door neighbour, and she was amazing. She had two sons, Peter and David, who went on to play rugby for the county, and she was incredibly generous with her time, driving me about when Mum couldn't. All my relatives were drafted in to help, as Mum tried to make sure I got wherever I needed to go, while still allowing her to do all the work she needed to do on the farm.

Once I was in the south-west side, we'd compete against the south-east which meant travelling to London and Middlesex a great deal. Then there was to be a south team to compete against a north team, so there were trials between possibles and probables to see who would play in that. I think Mum must have been praying I didn't get selected, because the higher I rose, the harder the work she'd have to put in to get me there. I'm very grateful to her, though. There's no question in my mind that she is a huge part of my success.

All these trials and country-related matches were on top of the games I was playing for the school against other local schools, and for Bude. It meant that I was playing two or three times a week. Hard for Mum, but great for me! That was the way you got on when I was younger; it's all changed now with the introduction of academies.

When I was a teenager I was playing three games a week and meeting loads of new players from all over the country all the time. I was meeting a host of selectors and coaches and getting my name known around the country. I was shoulder-deep in rugby and loving it. But it's not like that any more. An academy player, once he's signed by a club, might go through the season playing just a couple of matches in total and his whole time is spent training. If he's signed as a prop by a club, and the first-team prop goes through the whole season without injury or problem, he doesn't get to play. Then, because he hasn't played for ages, he ends up out of the academy and no use to anyone. I think the old way was better – let guys prove themselves first, and sign them when you're ready to play them, rather than have them in your academy so no one else can have them, and hope they'll be ready to play for you someday soon.

CHAPTER THREE:

PROGRESSING TO REDRUTH

Things were going well at Bude – my rugby was improving and I felt I was getting recognition with my selection for England U16s. I certainly wasn't looking to move on or to be promoted to a higher-ranking side, I was quite happy ticking along at my local club.

Anyway, my priority back then was the farm. When I finished at Budehampton School aged 16, I continued preparing for my life as a farmer. There was much I still had to learn and do ... I wanted to qualify as a cattle inseminator. Now this may sound like an odd thing to want to do, but all farms are looking to save money and we thought we could make savings if I did the inseminating, instead of paying for an outside company to do it for us. It was the only way to make the business work. The daft thing was that I got the qualification but then ended up leaving the farm before I ever got to use it on any of our cows!

I also sat my tractor test when I was 16, meaning I was qualified to drive the tractor on the road and annoy all the traffic forced to queue behind me, trying to get past. I had to go to a small training place, just through the village, to take my test. It wasn't too onerous an assignment for someone who'd been riding in tractors since he was a baby and driving them around on the farms since he could walk. I passed the test and it seemed that my future in farming was really starting to take shape.

I had left school in early summer 1992, so no longer had to worry about schoolwork and could throw myself into life on the farm. Then, one day, out of the blue, I had a call from a guy called Simon Blake. He said that he and a friend of his – a guy called Terry Pryor – would like to come and see me. I told them that was fine, but that I had milking to do, so they arranged to come over one evening in early July to have a chat with me. I remember the whole thing vividly. The two of them appeared at the farm in a Peugeot 205 and came into the house. They sat down and said they were coaches from Redruth Rugby Club, and had driven the hour-and-a-half trek to try and persuade me to come and play for the team – a much bigger club playing tougher opposition but based around 70 miles from my home. It turned out that Terry Pryor was a school teacher as well as being the club coach, and he knew of me through the school system because he had coached me at U14 level.

To be honest, my first thought when they asked me was that I was extremely flattered to be approached by the coaches from a much bigger club than the one I was playing for, but then I thought, *How on earth am I going to do that?* Redruth was miles away and I had cows to milk and a farm to help look after, and I couldn't drive (well, only a tractor). They were quite insistent, though, and said that playing rugby at a higher level would help my career develop.

I went to bed that night thinking about what to do. The more I thought about the proposition, the more eager I became. In the end, I decided to give it a go and play rugby for Redruth. I know that Bude weren't very happy when I told them, but I think they understood that I had to do this in order to progress.

So there began a very hectic part of my life when I was doing incredibly long days. My day would start with milking the cows at 5 a.m., then I'd be out on the farm all day. In the evening I'd do the milking, then Mum would come and pick me up to take me to Redruth for training. I'd jump into the car still wearing my milking gear and she'd have prepared my tea for me to eat on the way. I'd get there, slip out of my milking gear and into my rugby kit and go training.

Poor Mum would be left wandering around on the touchline, or sitting in the car, then she'd drive me home. She would do this twice a week and at the weekend, as well as driving me to loads of trials and representative matches. I know that other members of my family would help out with the trips at weekends – with aunts and uncles calling in to take me to the Midlands for trials and to London for matches and training weekends – but when I look back, so much of the ferrying around was done by Mum in her little car. I even remember that when I reached 17 and was learning to drive, I would drive there with L-plates on, with Mum in the passenger seat making sure we arrived in one piece.

The rugby at Redruth was a big step up after Bude but it was all made easier to adjust to because I found the club very welcoming, just as Bude had been when I'd first gone down there, aged 13. The first training session that I went down to at Redruth was in mid-August and it was held at Redruth School. The guys who were there at the time say it was very funny, because I arrived a little bit late for the session (all the milking and farming followed by the long journey to get there meant I was often late for things), so I turned up at the school and everyone else was already there. They say that they looked up as I appeared over this small hill leading down to the pitch, and for a moment, as I came into view, I appeared to totally block out the sun.

'It was like a scene from a film,' Simon told me. 'I had this tingling feeling; I knew we had someone special when I saw you arrive that time.'

It's great of the guys to have thought that, but I knew that even if the coaches and senior players thought I was something special, the regular team players wouldn't be so excited to see me because if I was successful it would mean that I would take someone else's place in the team. I would have to do a lot to persuade them that I was capable of contributing something that would help the club as a whole, and could slot into the team without making waves. Today, players come and go in teams all the time, but back then few people moved from team to team. You just played for the team in your town and that was that.

I got my chance to prove my worth to the players at the next Redruth training session which was held at

Cornwall College, in the third week of August. Now we were actually going to get stuck into a bit of rugby, rather than do fitness and skills as we had in the first sessions. I was introduced as this powerful U16 player who was the best thing since sliced bread. The captain of the side was a U19 player who was also a prop. He looked at me – I could see he didn't rate me – and I looked at him. The whole session descended into a power struggle between the two of us in which neither took a backward step all the way through the training session. We tested each other to the full. As an induction or initiation, it was unbelievable. After it, I found myself much more readily accepted by the guys because they knew that, in the heat of a match, I had the guts to keep going and keep fighting and would never let the team down.

It was important to me that they accepted me and realised that I was genuine and would play my heart out for the club. I'm a loyal sort of a guy, and once I was playing for Redruth I did my best to make sure I got to all the training sessions and matches I could and always took a step further than everyone else. I felt I had more to prove and wanted to show them that I was worthy of my place in the team. It was hard sometimes because if we hadn't finished on the farm I couldn't go to training, so I became determined not to let anything else, other than farming, interfere with my sport. My social life went out of the window, and life, to me, was farming and Redruth.

I remember there was a club tour to a place called Barkers Butts near Coventry that I was due to be going on, but then I got a call from John Elliott in the England set-up trying to get me to come to a final England trial. I didn't want to let Redruth down, so I went on the tour. I don't think any of the guys at Redruth could believe it, but I felt it was the right thing to do and I think I went up in their estimation afterwards. There was a part of me that thought, *If I'm good enough to play for England, I'll play for England*, without me having to let all my team-mates down in the process. Anyway, I don't think the England selectors held it against me because I was selected to play for England despite not going to the trial.

Farming continued to be an important part of my life and take up a great deal of my time. I remember telling my mates at Redruth that I couldn't come out at the weekend because I had to milk the cows. They looked at me oddly, as if they thought it was strange that I would be working at the weekend. No matter how many times I tried to explain about the twenty-four-hours-a-day, seven-days-a-week nature of farming, I don't think some of them ever quite got it. They thought I needed a break from work and a chance to let my hair down and have some fun; they didn't realise that's exactly what rugby offered. I valued their friendship enormously and always enjoyed my time down at the club.

In fact, if the truth be known, I enjoyed my time down at the club a little too much and I used to like a pint and a cigarette after a match. I remember one committee member saying to me, 'You'll have to cut back on that Guinness if you're ever going to make anything of your-self.' He probably had a point, and lucky I did cut back on it ... a bit.

When I first joined Redruth I was in the Colts but I didn't spend long there, and in November 1994 I played my first game for the first team, running out against Leeds at loosehead prop in National Division Four.

We lost that match 16–10, which was disappointing, but everyone told me I'd done well so that made up for it a little. I was playing out of position (loosehead instead of my usual tighthead) which didn't help, but I've gone through my career happy to play on both sides of the scrum, so it was probably useful practice at an early age. It was a great experience and my first away trip. One of the things I remember about the game was the physicality of it all. I remember this guy stamping on my head. It seemed to me that the opposition stamped and fought all the way through the match. I'd never known anything like it. It was like a big fight out there.

But my overriding memory is not of them stamping and fighting but of the Redruth guys coming to my rescue. I saw the way they piled in to save me, and got a real insight into what rugby is all about. I realised then that on the rugby field you're not alone. We were all there for each other. I remember that lesson today. To play an individual sport at the highest levels may give you a real buzz, but to me nothing beats a team sport like rugby in which you're all in it together. If things are going badly for you, someone will step in and help you; if things are going badly for someone else, you'll hurl yourself in to help them.

The funniest memory I have of that day is of walking back into the Leeds clubhouse, and seeing some old guy sitting at the bar. He had his pint in one hand and had already ordered another pint next to it as I walked in. He handed it to me as soon as I reached the bar, and said,

'There you go, mate. Well done. Good match today.' I looked at him, looked at the pint and shook his hand. Again it was a lesson in what rugby is all about. It made me laugh at the time that this team had just kicked the shit out of me and were now offering to socialise with me, and buy me a drink. I was 17 years old and I smiled to myself. Another little lesson in what it takes to be a great rugby player.

I stayed at Redruth for the rest of the season, playing the next eight or nine games on the trot, then came an offer that I really couldn't refuse. Gloucester Rugby Club were on the phone; they wanted me to come and join them. I never planned to leave Redruth, as I'd never planned to leave Bude before them, but sometimes life comes along and throws an offer at you that's too good to turn down. Gloucester were a big-time rugby club. It would be mad not to give it a go ...

CHAPTER FOUR:

GLOUCESTER WOES

To the outside world, it looked as if life was really coming together for me. I was a big, tough 19-year-old with the rugby world at my feet, and I'd been offered a chance to play at Gloucester. This was the big time. I packed my car with all my possessions, waved goodbye to everyone and everything that had ever meant anything to me, and headed north. I was going to play first-class rugby. I was off to the city. My big moment in life had arrived.

But Christ almighty I was terrified. Absolutely bloody terrified. Gloucester? That was a big f-ing scary place. I was this kid from a dairy farm in Cornwall. What the hell was I doing going to the big city? I didn't like big cities. I liked farms and cows. It was all wrong.

And yet, I went – driven by some need to fulfil the potential that others saw in me, and to be the great player that so many people were telling me I was destined to become. By the time I arrived in Gloucester, in the summer of 1995, I was hoping that it couldn't possibly be as bad as I feared it would be. I'd been building it up into something terrible. It wasn't. It was a lot bloody worse!

I hated it. I loathed it. As soon as I arrived I thought, *This is the biggest mistake of my life. What the hell am I doing here? Why did I come?* I was desperate to be back down in Cornwall with the people I loved, playing rugby for a club that I knew, having beers with my mates and enjoying life. Redruth was a great club. *What was I doing here? Why had I done this?*

The answer was Phil Greening. I had met Phil through the England schools set-up and the two of us got on straight away. He is such a great guy – very funny and doesn't take himself too seriously – we had a lot in common and we became good friends. Because I was coming up from Cornwall for schoolboy trials, coaching sessions and matches, it was always a long trek to wherever we were going, so I would often travel to Gloucester and stop off there to break the journey, staying with Phil's parents over-night, going out with Phil, then travelling on the next day with him. It meant the two of us becoming close friends, and me getting to know him and his parents very well.

His parents invited me up to Gloucester for the last game of the 1994–5 season because it was to be Mike Teague's last game and Phil's first game for the club. Teague had been one of my heroes growing up – a big, uncompromising player whom everyone hated playing against. He was a tough West Countryman. I identified with him. I liked the idea of heading up to Gloucester to watch Teague and cheer him along in his final game, while being there to support Phil in his first game, so off I went for the weekend.

My memories of the game aren't so good now and I'm struggling to remember whether Phil played well or badly (I'm assuming he did quite well since he went on to have a bloody good career there). I know it was a match against Harlequins and that Harlequins were fighting off relegation so it was a big game for them (they eventually won and stayed up), and every game's a big game for Gloucester, so it was a massive occasion.

What I remember most of all was that around 9,000 fans turned up to watch the game. I couldn't believe it. At Redruth we only had a couple of hundred for most games, and maybe 1,000 at the most. Here there was a big crowd cheering, stamping, singing and shouting during the game, and all staying behind to socialise afterwards. It was loud, colourful, bright and bloody wonderful, and all very different from anything I'd experienced before. I remember the adrenaline rush whenever a Gloucester player got the ball, and the whole stadium would rise in excitement and anticipation. I was hooked.

John Fidler was the manager of Gloucester at the time and I remember chatting to him in the bar afterwards. He asked me all about my rugby career, and where I thought my future lay, and I talked to him about Redruth and what a great club it was, and how much I was enjoying my rugby down there. Then he asked me what I wanted to drink.

'Cider, please,' I replied.

'I see. You'll fit in well here,' he said with a smile. So they obviously knew then that they wanted me to join the club, though I didn't know that at the time.

One of the ciders had the trademark GL on the bottle. I remember asking what the GL stood for, and John said,

'The GL stands for Gloucester lager, son.' He clearly said it as a joke, but I admit that for years I thought that stuff was called Gloucester lager! By the end of the evening I was completely bladdered on this newly discovered lager and enjoying a good night with the Gloucester boys.

It was soon after that game that I had a call from John, saying that Gloucester were very interested in me coming to play for them. I wasn't at all sure whether it was what I wanted to do and the prospect of moving away from home was quite worrying, but I did know Phil well, and I knew that it was a great club, so I sat down with Mum and talked the whole thing through. Then she said something that made me think it might not be so bad after all.

'If you don't like it, you can just come home – it's no problem. If you don't go, you'll never know what could have been.'

That seemed to be such a sensible point of view. It was great to be offered the chance to play alongside some of my childhood heroes, and in matches, week in week out, against the best players in the country. That's what I wanted to be doing. I would be insane not to give it a go, and Mum was right, I could always come back if I didn't like it.

So I accepted their offer of a chance to play for the club and was delighted to hear that they had also organised a job for me on a local farm with Ben Pullen, a huge Gloucester fan who owned a farm nearby. There was a flat that came with the place in the team and the job on the farm, and a car too. It seemed perfect for me. I'd be doing the things I enjoyed doing but at a much higher level, so that's why I made the journey to Gloucester to start my new life that summer.

It's hard to say, looking back, why it was that I hated it so much when I first arrived, but I think it was the feeling of isolation and the horrible unfamiliarity of it all. I'd sit there, desperately miserable, wondering why on earth I had moved. When you come from a small village, and particularly, I guess, when you are from a farming background, you take some time to adjust to life in a relatively big town. Phil Greening's parents were fantastic to me throughout this time. I thought about quitting and going home so many times, but they persuaded me to stay and told me that things would get better.

The trouble was, things didn't seem to get better. There were lots of times, and I mean lots of times, when I couldn't stand it any more and drove back down the M5 in the direction of Cornwall. I'd get home and Mum would have to talk me into going back to Gloucester, and she'd run through with me the many, many reasons why I should stay there. I know that was extremely difficult for her to do, because she would very much have liked me to stay in Cornwall on the farm, but she knew that the best thing for me would be to go back to Gloucester and give it a good shot. So time and again I would get into my car and drive back, only to get there and wish I was back in Cornwall. It was an extremely difficult time.

It was all the little things that I found difficult. For example, at home on the farm, I'd never had to go shopping at Sainsbury's or anywhere like that. I didn't buy food or go to the bank. I didn't have to buy any household things or think about bills or making sure there was food in the kitchen. All those things that other people took for granted were completely alien to me. And coupled with the loneliness I was feeling, and a great sense of homesickness, it made life very difficult.

Then, there was the club. I'll be honest, initially I didn't feel very welcome there. The guys at Gloucester weren't used to new players just turning up, and they didn't take to me at all. Guys didn't speak to you at Gloucester. It was very different from Redruth where I was right at the top of the tree and knew lots of people. Gloucester was very insular and an outsider coming in to Gloucester was unheard of. Back then, players didn't move to new clubs like they do now, and most of the guys there were Gloucester through and through – born and bred in the place. They didn't like some young whippersnapper coming in and taking up the coach's time and potentially taking a valuable place in the team. They were resistant to change and wanted everything to stay as it was.

For a year and a half at Gloucester I was under the radar. I think when I first moved to the club I was fifth-choice prop because there were so many props around. Because I wasn't one of the leading players, I was expected to act as gopher to the rest of the players during that first year. As the young lad in the set-up I was expected to be the carrier ... making cups of tea, carrying bags, rushing around after the other players. Anything that needed doing, I did it. It was a rung culture. You had to work your way up and earn people's respect before inching your way up the ladder.

I was working on the farm as well as playing at the club, because the sport was amateur in the early summer of

1995 (or 'shamateur', as it became known ... they couldn't pay you to play because the sport was, officially, amateur, so they would fix you up with a job, a flat and provide you with a car that was usually given to the club from a friendly local garage eager to support them). But it wasn't to stay amateur for much longer, and in August that year, when I had just arrived at Gloucester and was struggling to cope in my new environment, the sport was thrown into chaos by the decision in Paris to turn rugby from an amateur into a professional game. There had been a great deal of debate about whether the sport should remain amateur or turn professional, and many players had expressed strong feelings that the sport needed to become professional in order to develop, but despite the fact that the debates had been going on for years it still took us all by surprise when the announcement came through that rugby was to become a professional game.

The response at Gloucester was swift, as they appointed Mike Coley as the Club's first chief executive. The appointment of Richard Hill as director of rugby followed a month later as everyone involved in rugby set about trying to work out what being a professional sport really involved. Did it mean that we should train all day every day? Or just carry on doing the same training we had been doing? It was all very unclear. The confusion about what professionalism meant to the players was compounded by the fact that a moratorium year was imposed, meaning that we couldn't be paid by clubs for the first year of professionalism. None of us had a clue what was going on.

I must admit that the whole idea of rugby being professional confused me. I didn't associate playing rugby with work. I was in it for a love of the sport. When I'd stood there in Pontypridd, listening to the national anthem belting out while wearing an England U16 rugby shirt for the first time, proud beyond measure, it didn't occur to me that someone should be paying me. I'd been moved beyond words by the experience, and judged it to be bigger and more precious to me than any money that anyone could ever pay me. Rugby was about commitment, fearlessness and playing alongside men who you trusted and admired. It wasn't about salaries.

What I didn't realise at the time, and could never have realised, was that rugby turning professional would have the most astonishing impact upon my career. It couldn't have been better timed. There are lots of things that determine how your life will develop, lots of little things that happen along life's path that turn out to have huge consequences. This was one of them. I was extremely lucky to have joined a club like Gloucester at just the moment when the sport became professional, because what happened was that the whole focus of rugby changed and it became a time for sweeping out the old and bringing in the new. The players at Gloucester who'd hung onto their places and would keep their spots in the team regardless of how hard they trained or how often they turned up for fitness sessions, were cast aside.

It was a pivotal moment for rugby as it looked forward to a bright, shiny, commercial future. And for a 19-year-old who was feeling frustrated and fed up and in need of a big break, it was definitely a case of being in the right place at the right time.

CHAPTER FIVE:

TURNING PRO AT KINGSHOLM

The turning point for me and Gloucester, and the moment when I started to enjoy playing rugby rather than disliking everything about my new life, was when I realised, truly realised, what a big deal rugby was for the locals, and what a huge passion people had for the sport in the area. I think when I first got there I had my head down and was training and working hard, trying to cope in an alien environment which I didn't think suited me, but when I lifted my head, looked around and saw that the town was full of rugby nuts who really wanted the team to win, I started to come round a bit and to think that this might actually be a good place to play rugby.

Gloucester is a relatively small town, despite my initial view that it was a big city, and it comes alive on match days. Rugby is a big part of people's lives and supporters know the names of the players, and understand the sport inside out and back to front. They can debate all the finer points of tactics and team play with you, and they know exactly who they think should be in the team, and who they feel, very strongly, should not be in the team.

I remember walking into a pub in Gloucester and everyone turning round to look at me. Their eyes followed me as I walked through to the bar. When I got there, the barman stuck his hand out and shook my hand and welcomed me, and the locals wouldn't let me buy a drink. They really enjoyed being able to talk about rugby to someone in the team, and chat about how I thought Gloucester would get on that season.

I loved the people of Gloucester because I realised they were *my* people. Like those who I'd grown up with back in Bude, they were decent, hard-working guys who enjoyed their rugby and a few pints on a Saturday night. Most of them watched Gloucester play at the weekend but were also involved in the small clubs in the area – clubs that were exactly like Bude. I realised I was among good people who I could relate to and wanted to do well for. They were builders, carpenters, butchers, farmers – the sort of people for whom tickets weren't cheap, and who were making a big sacrifice to support the team. I felt I wanted to do well for them.

The supporters react with passion whenever Gloucester play, especially if the opponents are rivals and neighbours, like Bath or Bristol. If you do well, they adore you; if you don't play well for their beloved Gloucester side, heaven help you. In the week leading up to a match the excitement in the town rises to fever pitch. It's a challenge, a mighty challenge, and I felt suddenly very up for that challenge.

My first game for Gloucester was against Bath. In the Bath team at the time were players like Dave Hilton, John Mallett and Steve Ojomoh. These were guys I had seen on television who were now going to be playing against me. It was a second-team game, but we still had 6,000 people there to watch, which was roughly six times as many people as I'd played in front of before.

I found that I loved the banter and the fierce support of the guys in the infamous Shed. I enjoyed meeting the supporters afterwards and feeling part of something that mattered to people. The more my attitude changed, and I started enjoying rugby and working hard at it, the more I enjoyed being in Gloucester. Suddenly the dark days were behind me and I was starting to really enjoy my rugby ... and my life.

The other great memory that stands out for me about Gloucester is of the number of children involved in the club. There were always children around, involved in the youth section, supporting the players, hunting for auto-graphs. It gave the club a really nice feel.

I wanted to play well and to get into the first team. There was still a lot of home-grown talent playing at Gloucester, so if I was going to work my way into the team, and into the affections of the supporters, I needed to be good. I realised that I'd been drifting and not getting really stuck into training. I needed to work very hard to get myself noticed by Richard Hill and be given a chance in the main side. Once I started putting the hours in, training hard, and embracing the lifestyle, I started to love the place, the people and the rugby club even more.

While I was working hard at Gloucester, the rugby world was continuing to change all around me. Professionalism was getting its teeth into the sport and the game was being shaken to its core. It took a while to get to grips with what was needed in a professional game. To start with we assumed that you just needed more of what we were doing in the amateur days. It transpired that we needed to do things differently and become professional in our outlook as well as our training. I can remember thinking that I didn't want to be someone who was stuck in the gym all day building the body beautiful; I wanted to create the best chances for myself as a rugby player. I didn't want to be mindlessly exercising all day every day just because it was a professional sport and that's what we thought we should do. Soon fitness, diet and exercise professionals came in to the club who understood this, and worked on specific regimes for each of us with exercises that would make us better players.

As the club continued to mould itself into a professional club and get rid of a lot of players, I was one of the ones that they kept. It must have been tough for some of the older guys who'd been there for a long time. They now found themselves being put out to pasture because the game started to change all around them and a level of commitment was expected from them that they were unwilling or unable to give.

Being a 19-year-old who'd played England Colts and had his whole career ahead of him, I was kept on by the club and told that I had a great future if I trained hard and worked hard. I signed a contract with Gloucester and my career as a professional rugby player began. It wasn't for a life-changing amount of money: my first professional contract was worth £6,000–£8,000 at the time, so I wasn't out buying penthouse flats or sports cars, but it did mean that the club had a commitment to me and I had a commitment to them.

I was willing to buckle down and put the hours in at training in an effort to be the best player I could, but I definitely wasn't obsessed with making it right to the top. I always had a balance in my life that meant seeing my family and spending time with my friends were just as important to me as rugby. That part of me hasn't changed, despite the fact that I made it to the top echelons of rugby. I'm a strong believer that sport is more than just about playing well on the pitch. I don't think that training twenty-four hours a day, seven days a week, makes you a better player. It might make you fitter, arguably, but it won't necessarily make you a better or more refined player on the pitch. If you're happy in yourself and having fun, that will carry over into your rugby life.

Once I had my professional contract under my belt, I could leave my job and become a full-time rugby player. It was quite a big moment for me because I'd always thought that I would make my money in life as a farmer. I never, in a million years, envisaged the changes in the sport that would allow me to make money from rugby instead of farming.

But it wasn't all easy-going. My first league game was against Harlequins, away, in late 1996, and we lost by about 50 points. It was awful. This was in the days when Richard Hill had one team for home games and another team for away games. We got absolutely battered. Keith

Wood, Jason Leonard and Will Carling were playing for Quins back then, so they had a good side, but it was still awful to lose to them by so many points.

I remember vividly the disappointment I felt at losing so badly, knowing what it meant to the people of Gloucester. I couldn't imagine what the reaction would be when they found out how badly we'd lost the match. We travelled back to Gloucester in the coach and arrived back at the clubhouse. I can remember walking up the road in Gloucester and saying to the guys I was with that I didn't want to go out that evening.

'I'm just going to head straight home,' I said, but Tony Windo, Gloucester's captain, spun round, looked me right in the eye and said, 'You will not go home. You will come out. You f-ing will go out. You've got nothing to be ashamed of. You will hold your head up and go out. You've played your best today.'

I'll never forget that. Tony Windo was a real good guy and he taught me that day that you have to do your best, and that's all you can do. Of course it was important to win and of course the people of Gloucester were much happier with the team if we won, but that didn't mean that we were never allowed to lose, and if we did we should hide ourselves away.

I knew that it wasn't my fault that we lost by so many points, but the thing with playing for a team like Gloucester is that you do take everything personally and the thought of going out drinking in the town was a bit frightening. In the end, though, after Tony had words with me, I went out that night after all and I got a bit of stick but nothing much. I suppose, back then, many people didn't really know who I was, so didn't realise I'd been playing for Gloucester that day.

By the time people do know who you are, and recognise you in the street and give you grief for the way you played, at least you're experienced enough to deal with it. This has been one of the interesting things about fame, for me. People think you become famous overnight, but it's not like that. As you play more and get more recognised, you get more press then more people know you. Then you play for England you get a bit more attention, then the Lions, and get a bit more attention, then you start winning for England and people want to start writing about you, then you win the World Cup and get even more attention.

Fame happens gradually so you get used to it; you slowly become accustomed to the fact that more and more people know who you are. You grow with it and it becomes normal.

Having said that, I think you get local fame much quicker in a place like Gloucester where they're rugby crazy than you would in other places. If you're a rugby player, you can't do anything in Gloucester without people knowing all about it. The place is a rumour mill. Even if you didn't do it, you probably did! Everyone knows everyone's business. It's nice in many ways but it does mean that you can't ever escape from rugby. That's what comes of being in a rugby town. That's what I learnt. You have to take it on the chin.

As well as the on-the-field rugby changing as a result of professionalism, things were changing in the organization of the club as well, and in April 1997 Tom

Walkinshaw came on board as Gloucester's new owner. He was immensely rich and had a proven pedigree in sport through his work with Formula One, so was considered to be the ideal person to lead us through the change to becoming a fully professional club. You tend to forget that rugby becoming a professional sport made a huge impact on the administration of the clubs as well as the players.

The clubs had been ticking over previously, taking in sponsorship money at a fairly low level and using it to make minor alterations to the grounds and pay a skeleton staff. Now, suddenly, the clubs needed to make a lot of money to pay the players properly. If they couldn't pay the players decent salaries, other clubs who'd found millionaire backers would step in and sign them up. Every club needed a rich individual, and preferably one with good business sense, to keep them afloat while the sport went through its transition to professionalism.

The year that Tom Walkinshaw came in was the same year that I went on a Canadian tour with the Colts which raised my profile down at the club and through the rugby world generally. This was heightened when I played my first England A game.

England A was a huge step up for me. I hadn't been at Gloucester long, so was still adjusting to the step up that involved. Now I was in the England A team. Back then, England A was a bigger stepping stone than it is now; it was the definite link level between the clubs and the England team and few people would find themselves playing for England without first playing for England A.

The first game was an ERC (England Rugby Clubs) XV v New Zealand game at Ashton Gate, Bristol's ground. They had Sean Fitzpatrick and Olo Brown in the side. I couldn't believe it; I'd be playing against my childhood heroes. There's something so amazing about taking the field against people you've admired from when you were a young boy. Olo Brown was immense – he had this huge presence on the field. Scrummaging against him was an awesome experience because he just doesn't go anywhere. He's solid.

The other great experience was seeing the haka up close. I'm a big fan of these rugby traditions and it was great to see it being done right in front of me. I stood on the pitch with my great heroes in front of me, watching the haka with 20,000 people in the crowd – unbelievable. A real privilege. On my side, there were Dave Sims, the Gloucester captain, and Tim Rodber, another great hero of mine.

Clive Woodward had become England coach and had got rid of the old guard, so guys like Rodber who'd had fantastic careers had fallen into the A-team on their way down. Rodber would bounce back and be in contention for the 1999 World Cup, but at that moment he was being tested by Woodward to see if he had what England needed. It was such an honour to run out alongside him and the other A-team players. I spent the whole time listening carefully and learning. I was like a sponge trying to soak up every bit of information and to benefit from everything I was hearing from these guys who'd been there and done it. Looking back, the selection for England A was a crucial moment in my life, and a big break for me because it would mark the start of my career really taking off.

The second A-game was at Welford Road, home of Leicester and their fortress when it came to club rugby. It was great to go there and not be booed and jeered by them all. It was here that I ended up getting the nickname 'Raging Bull'. The name came about because Mark Allen, the New Zealand prop, was known as the bull, and apparently when he played at home everyone made the noise of a bull and would shout, 'The bull's in the farmyard!' when he ran out. In order to counteract that, Clive Woodward said, 'Well, we've got a raging bull here, his name's Phil Vickery.' Because I was brought up on a farm, the guys loved that name for me, and it stuck. There were obviously lots of farmyard references from my teammates and much laughter as they all took to calling me by my new name. But I grew to like being called Raging Bull and I've even called my range of clothing after it, and this book!

Welford Road was an amazing place to play because we had all this support. It's not a great place to go when you're playing against Leicester, because obviously you have very little support from the crowd, but I do remember how great it was when we went there with England and had them all on our side.

There's no doubt that my stock rose as a result of playing for England A and I learnt something that I'd never realised before – that life is very competitive when you rise through the ranks. Suddenly I was the person to beat, the person that other props wanted to do better than in matches because I was the young, up-and-coming

England prop. I remember playing Bath soon after the England A game and John Mallett was chasing me around, and working hard to look better than me. I knew I'd have to up my game. I felt I had to prove myself every time I played. People were looking at me as the guy knocking on the England door, not as the friendly, slightly tubby farmer who'd come on up from Cornwall. I was being taken seriously by other people and I had to start taking myself seriously. Well, not too seriously, because I'd never do that, just more seriously than I had done up until that point.

CHAPTER SIX:

ENGLAND CALLING

After the fantastic experience of playing for England A at Welford Road, it was back to Gloucester with a series of tough matches one after another. The standard of rugby being played in clubs had already begun to improve since the arrival of professionalism. Defences were harder to penetrate and players were starting to get fitter. The game was tougher than ever.

I remember playing in a particularly hard-fought match against Leicester at Kingsholm. Back then they had Richard Cockerill, Martin Johnson, Neil Back and a plethora of international players in their side. They had a particularly good pack so I knew I would have my work cut out. In this match in early February I remember the scrum going down badly, and the referee telling us to stand up. As I did so, Graham Rowntree gave me an uppercut right into the side of my jaw. Bloody hell it hurt. I still remember the pain today. I managed to get through the rest of the match and woke up to a very sore jaw the next morning. I decided that next time I saw Graham Rowntree he'd pay for that punch.

A couple of days later, I was at home one afternoon when I had a call from John Fidler. He told me that the England coach had been on the phone and wanted me to go to the Petersham Hotel in Richmond to join the international rugby team. 'They want you to play for England,' he said. 'You've done it, son. Well done!'

I suppose I should report that the world spun on its axis as soon as John said those words, but the truth is that I was so worried about how on earth to get to this hotel in London that I didn't have time to get excited about my selection for the national side. I know that for most people winning an international cap would be a most special moment in their lives, so I wish I could describe it as being thrilling and exciting but, genuinely, the only thing going through my mind was ... *London? I don't want to drive to London. How on earth will I get there? Where is London? Which motorway do I take? The M3? Where's that?*

I asked John where I had to go and he told me to head to south-west London. *Christ, where was that?* I was given a map and told which motorways to take, and I was sent on my way.

Eventually, I got there. I arrived at this magnificent old hotel called the Petersham, grabbed my bag from the boot of the car and walked into the marble reception area. I didn't know where to go, who to ask for or what to do. I hovered around, wondering who to approach when I saw Lawrence Dallaglio striding across the reception area towards me, and putting his hand out to shake mine. He welcomed me to the England hotel and he probably, to this day, has no idea how much that meant to me. I'd driven to a place I was unfamiliar with, late at night, to meet the best team of players in England, and to join them to play a level of rugby I wasn't familiar with. That friendly gesture from Lawrence made me feel welcome. It was a great thing to do.

Things didn't stay all that great though because when I got up to the room, still nursing my face from the punch I had received from Graham Rowntree when we had met across the scrum the previous Saturday, I discovered my room-mate was ... the same bloody Rowntree! I looked at him, this bloke who had given me a cheap punch in the face, and thought, *This is the last person in the world that I want to spend time with*. Seriously, though, Rowntree is a brilliant bloke and he was a great team-mate. He was a good room-mate too, but it was funny to see him standing there, welcoming me to my room, while I was still sporting the bruises he'd given me the last time I'd seen him.

It was difficult to turn up at the England team hotel, and mix straight in with this group of players who'd been together for a while, especially since none of them were from Gloucester, but what helped was the feeling of camaraderie from the other players. It had taken me just thirty-four first-team games for Gloucester before I was asked to join the England squad and my first match in England colours happened just eighty-one days after my England A début, so there was a great deal of talk about me, a lot of interviews to give, and press attention to cope with. I didn't even know whether I would be in the team to play France, or whether I'd just been brought in for cover at training.

I got through my first evening in the team hotel, and went out training with the players the next day. Bloody hell. I've always been a physical bloke, and I'd been playing a decent standard of rugby at Gloucester, and for England A, for a while, so I was fit and used to very hard rugby training, but – blimey – nothing like that! I knew that it would be a step up when I was called into the international squad, but it was rugby training on a whole different level. I just wasn't prepared for it and, I'll be honest, I almost died in the first scrummaging session. No, really, I did almost die. It was so bloody cold and we did so many scrums. Time and time again we were forced to reset the scrum and replay the moves. I couldn't believe what was going on. I was 23 stone of bright red beetroot for about a week afterwards. I think it took me about a year to get over that session. The reality of international rugby hit me like a sledgehammer, leaving me determined to lose weight, sharpen up and get properly fit to compete in this environment. It's interesting to look back now ... when I first turned up for that England training session I was 130kg; by the next Five Nations I was 115kg!

Playing for England was going to be hard. I'd had a taste of how hard it would be when I'd been selected to play for England A, so I was under no illusions. When you played for England at the time you came up against the Leicester mafia and as a lone guy from Gloucester I felt outnumbered from the start, but I always felt that if I worked hard my work would be rewarded. The culture with England at the time was a real can-do one, thanks to Clive's influence, and however out of sorts you felt, and however baffled by events, you knew that if you put in the effort and produced the goods Clive would be there to support you.

The game that I was drafted into the squad for was against France in Paris. I was told that I would be sitting on the bench. I was absolutely terrified. I spent the whole time hoping to God that I wouldn't have to go on to the pitch. I know that might sound odd, but remember, these were the days when if you were on the bench nobody really communicated with you, so I had no idea what was going on out there. I didn't even know what the lineout calls were. The idea of running onto the pitch in Paris to play against France in my first match for England, and not having a clue what anyone was doing or what their calls meant, was quite terrifying. I was happier just sitting out the match on the bench ...

Things have changed a great deal during my time with England, and one of the things that has changed enormously is the relationship between the bench players and the first XV. You feel as if you're very much part of the team when you're on the bench now, but back then it was as if you didn't exist. I suppose the crucial difference is that now when you're on the bench there's every chance you're going to get on to the field, whereas in the past you only went on to the field if there was an injury to someone, so it was less likely that you would be involved in the game. Today, bench players are absolutely vital because they are the players you bring on at crucial times in the game. Why would you ever put on a player who didn't even know the lineout calls? It seems ridiculous, looking back, but when I started, rugby was a very different game to the one played now. I'm not *that* old but it sometimes feels as if I played in two different sports – before and after professionalism had fully kicked in.

So, there I was, back in 1998, at a time when the England front five was very Leicester orientated, the only person in the squad from Gloucester, still recovering from the most terrifying training session I'd ever encountered, still bruised from when my now room-mate had punched me, sitting on the bench for England versus France with 80,000 people screaming at the pitch. I didn't know any of the moves and I didn't know the lineout calls. *Please don't let me on the pitch, please don't let me on the pitch*, I thought as play commenced. Happily, I didn't have to go on. Even today I think it's hard to come off the bench, with little warning, and give your best performance, especially if it's your first game and you have no idea what to expect when you get out there. From my point of view, I know I've never prayed so hard for anything as I prayed for Clive Woodward not to send me on to the pitch on that day in Paris. We lost the match, unfortu- nately, but the good news was that I was selected to play against Wales at Twickenham the following weekend. Not on the bench – on the pitch.

I arrived at the Petersham Hotel a week before the game against Wales (it was slightly easier this time – at least I knew where the hotel was) and met up with the other players. We had a training session on the Monday which nearly killed me again, and once again I vowed to lose weight when I saw my scarlet face in the mirror. On the Tuesday there was a big press conference at the hotel. All the journalists had come to hear the announcement of the team, then interview the players. I'd been warned that, as the new boy, everyone would want to interview me, but I hadn't realised just how excitable it would all become. I walked into the press room, after the team had been announced, and was immediately grabbed by journalists. It was fine, they just wanted to know how I felt and what I expected from the game, which Welsh players I was looking forward to coming up against ... things like that. I have never had a problem with the press but I did find it hard when I first had to do it because it is one thing that you are not prepared for.

Another thing you're not prepared for is all the attention you get. People calling me to see how I was, asking for tickets, giving me advice and suggesting popping in to see me after the match ... I learnt very quickly that all the attention can be distracting and draining. If you're not careful you can lose so much of your energy doing things other than rugby. I could have charged around trying to find tickets for people, replying to emails and doing every interview request made of me, but that would have used energy that I had to reserve for the match.

A lot of people asked me if I found it stressful in the lead up to the match. I don't think that 'stressful' is the right word to describe how I felt, because I have always been quite good at separating myself from the anxieties surrounding a match. I had found it difficult in Paris because I hadn't felt properly prepared, but usually I tell myself that it's just a piece of grass. It's the same size piece of grass as you play on every week. There'll be fifteen blokes one side, fifteen blokes on the other side. You do this week in week out, and just because everyone is making a fuss about it doesn't mean anything will be different when you're on that piece of grass.

You lose too much energy if you stress about things. The truth of the matter is that you have been selected because people believe that you are good enough to be out there, and if you're worried about it then the fear is in your head. You wouldn't be in the team if they were concerned about your ability. Now you have to get the confidence and believe you can do it, and go out there and do what everyone believes you are capable of doing. I know I'm making it sound simpler than it is, but you do have to have a train of thought like this to survive.

There were so many new things to get used to in the week leading up to a game ... new calls in the lineouts, not being familiar with the other players, different coaching styles. John Mitchell nearly killed me in his training sessions. I'm sure I must have gone green in every one of them. It was awful. But the game was so much faster that you needed to be much fitter than you had to be to play the club game.

The night before the match I managed to sleep a little by taking a sleeping tablet. I tend to have to do that before a big game because I'm a bit of a worrier. At 2 a.m. in the morning I'll be pacing around, reminding myself about the moves, the calls, and wondering how I'm going to pay the mortgage. Sleeping pills knock me out and ensure that I get the good night's sleep that is essential if you're going to play well at international level.

The thing I remember most clearly about the next morning and, indeed, the week leading up to the game is the number of letters, faxes, telegrams and emails that poured into the Petersham Hotel for me. Loads of people had taken the trouble to contact me, including Mike Teague, the former England player who'd been such a stalwart for Gloucester. I really cherished those letters and I'll take the opportunity now to say an enormous thank you to everyone who took the trouble to send them. I was really touched by notes from guys I knew at Bude and Redruth. It's difficult to get in contact with people to thank them at the time because there's so much going on, but it was humbling to get all those notes from people and I'm very grateful.

I suppose I didn't really know what a massive thing it was to play international rugby until I saw the letters and faxes and the interest caused by my selection. It just hadn't ever been this big dream of mine to get to the top of rugby, like it is for so many people. I was always the sort of guy who just concentrated on the game he was playing.

We made the short journey to Twickenham by coach, then headed into the changing room. My most enduring memory is of walking out of the tunnel; that was amazing. I came out onto the pitch when we first arrived and saw there were just a few people in the stands, then I went out to the team warm-up twenty minutes later and it was half full. I didn't go back out again after that, I stayed in the changing room and got myself taped up while some of the others went out to throw the ball around, so when I went out for the start of the game, just fifteen minutes later, it was packed in the stadium. It seemed astonishing that so many people had packed into the place in just a few minutes.

People talk about the noise when you run out of the tunnel, and it is truly amazing ... like a wall of sound that hits you as you run onto the pitch. Then there's the singing of the national anthem, which is such a highlight for me. I love it – there's sound, a loud, roaring noise, then suddenly you'll catch the words being sung and it all becomes so poignant.

I was given a great bit of advice in the lead up to the match that has stayed with me. Jason Leonard came over to me, looked me in the eye, and said, 'Make sure you enjoy what you're doing and live in the minute. It'll go so quickly; enjoy it all.' I decided to try and take Jason's advice, and as we dispersed after the anthems and prepared for the game, I was determined that I was going to enjoy this experience and cherish every minute.

Yeah. Great, in theory. It proved to be much harder than I'd imagined because it was so tough. After ten minutes I was blowing out of my arse! I was absolutely bloody knackered. I'd never known anything like it. I'd been warned about how fast the game would be, but it was way faster than I'd expected. It felt so incredibly furious. It was hard to see what was going on, and get a sense of what was happening on the pitch, when it was all flying past you at such a pace. The daft thing is that I bet if I looked back at the match now I'd laugh at how slow it was, but back then it was such a huge step up from what I was used to.

All my memories of the game are of the great speed and the big hits. Everyone seemed bigger, faster and more focused than I had ever seen in rugby before. I just had to concentrate on what I had to do and what my role was. I remember trying to stay in my zone and do what I was there to do, but things happen in international rugby that you don't expect and you're not experienced enough to cope with. They floor you temporarily, but you have to deal with them and get back on the game. If you make a mistake or someone does something you're not expecting, you have to keep a clear head and focus back on what your role is. I think that's one of the hardest things in international rugby – keeping your focus on what you need to do while chaos reigns all around.

The overwhelming feeling after that first cap was of just how proud I felt and how lucky I was to have the opportunity to have played the sport at that level with those guys. We all went to the Park Lane Hilton for a massive dinner and I remember being so excited to be at the Hilton. Scott Quinnell came over to see me. He'd given me quite a whack in the game, so he was the first person to come and have a drink with me. He gave me a glass of wine which I knocked back. He said, 'Well done,' then another Welsh player came up and did the same, then another, then another ...

Then all my team-mates came up ... one by one. I drank wine with them all. By the time the dinner started I was absolutely legless. Lawrence was captain so he stood up to speak, and I was so drunk I stood in the corner shouting, *'Bruno, Bruno, Bruno!'* (his middle name). Lawrence had to keep looking over and asking me to be quiet. The evening's all a bit vague after that, but I'm told that Jason Leonard and Roger Uttley carried me to my room and put me in the bathroom, with my head in the toilet. It wasn't the most dignified way to end my first cap, but it was a lot of fun. I woke up at 5 a.m. with a raging thirst and dried sick all over my hair and clothes. Horrific. Things didn't get any better when I found out that I'd been cited by Peter Boyle, the match commissioner, for punching Colin Charvis in the second half of the game. I must admit that the first thing I thought when I was told about the citing was, *What about Scott Quinnell punching me?*

When it came to the citing, I was lucky on this occasion, though, because it never amounted to anything. I was told that I would be penalised with a one-month suspension, which seemed harsh, because the offence would have meant me getting just a yellow card if it had been dealt with by the referee during the game. In the end, Roger Pickering, who was the Five Nations' chief executive at the time, changed Boyle's decision because he said, 'The citing procedure was not followed to the letter. There were misunderstandings between people who I have no intention of naming and as a result of the legal advice obtained by the committee the suspension was deemed unsafe.' All very odd, but I wasn't complaining.

I staggered out of that hotel in the morning, still drunk, I imagine, aching from head to foot and with the worst headache known to mankind, but I felt lucky. Very lucky. I'd been given the opportunity to play for my country. Now I needed to do everything possible to make sure that I was given the opportunity again.

CHAPTER SEVEN:

'IF I HAD A GUN, I'D SHOOT THE BLOODY LOT OF YOU'

I had played in the game against Wales at Twickenham because Darren Garforth, the first-choice tighthead prop, had been out through injury, and when he came back for the remaining games in the Five Nations Championships and took his place in the side I took my seat on the bench. It always takes a while to work your way into the affections of the England coach, so it was what I expected. Clive Woodward tended to be loyal to players whom he rated and wanted in his team, so I wasn't in the least surprised that Darren came back into the side.

We followed up the 60–26 victory over Wales with a 34–20 victory over Scotland at Murrayfield and a 35–17 victory over Ireland, to put us second in the table behind France who had beaten us in that first game (the one that I had watched, terrified, from the bench). It meant we won the Triple Crown, and I'd been part of it, which was fantastic.

I was on the England coach's radar now. Clive Woodward had seen me playing for England, and knew I'd coped well under pressure, so I hoped I would be given another opportunity to play soon.

Happily, that opportunity came in the summer of 1998. Sadly, it was on a tour that would always be referred to as 'The Tour from Hell' because of the absolute drubbing we received in every game we played. In a strange way it was the best thing that could have happened to the England team at that time, and could be regarded as one of the key reasons for England's victory in the World Cup in 2003 because it shoved us right down to the bottom and galvanised us to fight our way back up again.

The benefit of hindsight – isn't it a wonderful thing? I assure you that it didn't feel like the best thing to happen to England at the time. The tour was good but the matches were awful.

When I was told I had been selected to play, I was obviously delighted, but there was no doubt that it would be a tough series. The itinerary was incredible: we would have to play four Tests in five weeks over three continents in the southern hemisphere. It was a crazy tour to have been slotted between a Lions series and a World Cup, and Clive Woodward was keen to point out that it was something he had inherited when he became England coach the previous year, and not the sort of tour that he would have chosen to set up himself.

It was a tough enough assignment for the most experienced of players, and in 1998 we were significantly lacking experience. I'm sure I was chosen because I had two working legs. Many of the country's leading players, guys like Martin Johnson, Lawrence Dallaglio, Jason Leonard and Richard Hill, had picked up niggles over the season that they needed to get sorted in the summer, so they couldn't tour. With a World Cup the following year, none of the top players wanted to go into the 1998–9 season with injuries.

So the big names pulled out, leaving Clive to assemble a group of everyone else. He tried to convince the southern hemisphere coaches that England had strength in depth, and that losing almost every top player would not stop the team from being competitive, but the reality is that, in every country in the world, if you take away all the leading players it's hard to have a competitive team. In the end the squad that went on tour contained twenty uncapped players. It certainly didn't please Clive that he had to select players with little experience, and it didn't please the Australians either. To say they reacted strongly would be an understatement.

Dick McGruther, the Chairman of the Australian Rugby Union, attacked first, describing the England tour party as 'probably the most underequipped group of Englishmen to be sent to Australia since the first Fleet'. The Australians like to mouth off about things, but McGruther seemed to be genuinely upset that England were sending a team that could not be described as a 'best team'. England was accused of treating the southern hemisphere with contempt, and McGruther finished his attack by inviting all Australians to come and enjoy a 'Pommie thrashing'. All of this, and we hadn't yet stepped onto the plane. My first touring experience with England was clearly going to be a baptism of fire.

We arrived down under in late May, and realised straight away that McGruther wasn't alone in the criticisms he was expressing about us. The newspapers were full of condemnatory articles in which Australian journalists were laughing at us, and dragging up former players to join in with the mirth. We just wanted to play rugby, and to be given the chance to prove that we were good enough to wear the England shirt. The newspapers reported that only six players in our tour party had more than ten England caps to their name. The average was fewer than four. I had one, which was one more than ten other forwards and ten backs had.

But the impact of all the negative comment in the press, and the sniping at the England team, was to bind the team closer together, and push us to rely on one another and focus inward on the squad. The result of all this was that the tour was actually great fun, and we bonded very quickly. I was so enthusiastic about it all and dying to get stuck into the Australians who were criticising us so much. I knew there was a great deal of raw skill in the squad and I was relishing the fact that I had the opportunity to be here in the southern hemisphere, about to take on some of the world's best players.

The captain for the tour was Matt Dawson, who I got on extremely well with, and came to really admire. Daws is good fun but he's also a good leader. He had a group of players who had hardly any experience between them, but he brought them all together and made them feel like they could win. I enjoyed working with him, and gained a lot of respect for him on the trip.

The first match was against Australia, and we went down to a humiliating 76–0 defeat, featuring 11 Australian tries. There were a few good things to take from the defeat, like the fact that we didn't concede a try for more than half an hour, but there's no getting away from the fact that we were annihilated, and the victory for Australia served to confirm all their pre-match rantings about us.

John O'Neill, the Chief Executive of the Australian Rugby Union, said after the game, 'This is not what international rugby is about. It wasn't a contest. Those poor players, as determined and proud as they are, were not Test players.'

John Mitchell, our assistant coach, had a different take. He took one look at us after the game and said, 'If I had a gun I'd shoot the lot of you.' He then said that we had a chance to come back after this first defeat, on the New Zealand leg of the tour. He didn't want to see us losing any more matches, he said. The truth is that if we'd stayed down there for another ten years we wouldn't have won a game. They were simply better than us.

I think the main lesson we learnt from the defeat was just how far the Australians had moved on since professionalism, and it was an important lesson for us in that respect. No one knew quite what changes would be brought about when the sport lost its amateur status – well, now we had our answer. We had a lot of work to do to catch up with them, let alone beat them.

I learnt a lot on that tour. I learnt what great characters the England guys alongside me were. Even though we were being defeated every time we stepped onto a pitch, the guys stayed upbeat; there was no terrible blame culture and no moaning.

After that first Test we headed for New Zealand where we would have two further Tests, and we stopped off in Queenstown to have a few days' escape from the negative criticism. Clive said we could have a day off there to unwind and recover from the match and the terrible bashing we'd had in the press. 'Don't do anything silly,' were his parting words, as he left us to our own devices. The words stuck in my mind. I was a new boy; I wasn't going to do anything silly. The last thing I wanted was to lose my place in the side. Garath Archer was a different character altogether, though. That boy is a nutter, and the minute we were in Queenstown he was off to find where they did the first-ever bungee jump. He found the place, stripped naked and bungee jumped head first. I kept thinking, *What if Clive finds out?* but of course Clive didn't and everything was fine. I think we needed something daft like that to happen, to take our minds off the tour and the increasingly negative feedback we were getting as the tour progressed.

At the end of that week we played the All Blacks A team, coached by Graham Henry and featuring some big bloke called Jonah Lomu. There were no easy matches on this tour. The game was played in rain-lashed Hamilton. It was awful. But we did get stuck into them and restricted them to an 18–10 win. A defeat's a defeat, but at least it was an improvement. It was commented on how well the forwards had played too, which pleased me immensely. Clive said he thought the forwards had turned in a heroic performance in horrendous conditions. You have to take the praise when you can get it on a tour like that. And at least there was a funny moment to make us all giggle when Peter Richards turned up for the game without his boots. John Mitchell went absolutely bloody nuts.

Having been relatively pleased with our performance in Hamilton, we were brought right back down to earth in Invercargill when we lost to the New Zealand Academy. Things didn't bode well for the next big game.

The first New Zealand Test was in Dunedin, and we lost by a record score and margin, but the 64–22 scoreline doesn't begin to reflect the way we played. We got stuck in, in that match, in a way that belied our distinct lack of experience at that level. The All Blacks had all their big names. There was Craig Dowd, Norm Hewitt, Olo Brown, Robin Brooke, Andrew Mehrtens, Frank Bunce, Jonah Lomu ... I remember when they took Lomu off and I thought, *Thank God for that, at last we might have a chance here*, and then they brought on Joey Videri. Bloody Videri! It was just insane. There was no way through. No weak links.

We played the New Zealand Maoris next, and lost 62–14, then lost the second Test 40–10. It wasn't shaping up to be the most successful tour ever conducted by an English team but we were learning a great deal every day and gaining valuable experience, and while the headline writers sniped, I believed that I was turning into a better player with every match I played.

The truth is that you get stronger from the defeats. Of course, every player in the world would love to win every match he ever played, but the mental hardness and commitment you need to succeed at the top often comes from coping with defeat on the way, so losing is a vitally important part of winning. That's probably true about life as much as it is about rugby.

The tour was a really stark reminder, for everyone involved in English rugby, of just how much needs to be done to succeed at the highest level. Everyone knew they had to return from the tour and work harder than we'd ever worked before. We had all enjoyed ourselves, had done a lot of travelling, and we learnt just how much work we would have to do before the next World Cup. We realised how far behind we were, and I think sometimes you need to do that. You need everything to fall apart so that you really focus and throw yourself into the future. It was just a shame that the World Cup was the following year so we didn't have much time to make any changes.

The tour had also been a reminder to me of how precious England caps are and how hard I should work and how privileged I should feel to receive one. David Sims had got a cap, at last, after years of devotion to Gloucester and England, and we were all delighted for him. It made me think about how hard some guys have to work just to get one cap, and how I had stepped into the England team after relatively few games for Gloucester. I was lucky to have found myself in the England team at such a young age, and I was determined to enjoy every minute of it, and relish each cap. I also vowed to work harder and get fitter in an effort to keep being selected.

There had been fun along the way too, such as the time when we decided that Josh Lewsey, who earned his first cap on the tour, had a head of hair that was way too impressive for a rugby player. There was only one thing to do ... we held him down while a neat circle was shaved out of the top of his hair. He had a large bald patch in the middle of his head. He looked ridiculous. In short, it was perfect. Clive Woodward wasn't quite as impressed with our hairdressing skills as we were ourselves, though, and instructed him to get down to the barbers and have the rest of it cut. We were disappointed that our efforts with the scissors went to waste, but there was some joy when he returned from the barbers looking like a convict! That'll teach him for having such glossy, blond hair on tour.

The tour was not over after the New Zealand stage. From the island of the long white cloud we had to make a 28-hour journey to South Africa for two further Test matches. First we went to Cape Town where Clive did the infamous hotel switching, checking us out of the three-star team hotel we'd been booked into, and into the best hotel in South Africa, known locally as the Pink Palace, which was about six times the price. Clive paid for the hotel on his own credit card because he was so determined that England should be treated like professionals in order to bring out the very best in us, but since his gesture came in the middle of the least successful tour ever conducted by an England side it was not terribly well received by those at the RFU. Still, it gave us a great indication of the lengths that Clive would be willing to go to, to make sure the players were given every help possible to be the best they could.

In South Africa we were beaten 18–0 in Cape Town. The tour as a whole had been disappointing in so many ways – the results, and not least the shoes that we'd had to wear throughout. Clive had done a deal with a footwear manufacturer for us to get 'smart' new shoes to wear with our number one outfits for formal occasions. In truth, the shoes were mustard-coloured. Shoes shouldn't be mustard-coloured. It's possible that nothing in life should be mustard-coloured except mustard ... certainly not shoes. Anyway, we had our revenge on the odd foot-wear when we all threw them into the garden after the last game of the tour and burnt them. The sickly smell of burning leather and rubber is my final memory of the Tour from Hell. After that, we headed home – Clive to be admonished for moving us to a hugely expensive hotel, and the rest of us to think about the tour we'd just been on. There's no doubt that it was a bittersweet experience. It's never good to lose by those huge scorelines, but it was a great experience for all of us uncapped players who made the trip. I think the tour was a turning point in English rugby and, without it, guys like me wouldn't have been in the frame for the World Cup the following year.

CHAPTER EIGHT:

YOMPING WITH THE ROYAL MARINES

There was a real change in momentum in the England set-up once we got back from the summer tour, a real feeling that no one wanted England to suffer in the southern hemisphere like that ever again. I know that Clive was determined that things would change – he had a renewed sense of purpose and commitment to the team, and a conviction that if he got things right for England they could become world-beaters. Whatever your views of Clive, he never swayed from believing that England could be the best side in the world, and always did everything in his power to create an environment in which they could prove it.

The thing I liked a lot about Clive was the fact that he took personal responsibility for making sure that every-thing around the England team was as good as it could be. The incident in South Africa, when he had moved us to a better hotel because he was unhappy with the one we were in, was confirmation of that. In all his time with England he was looking for new and better ways of doing things, ways of allowing us to concentrate on playing the game and have everything else taken care of. I know some of Clive's ideas came over as being a bit bonkers, and there were times when all the players thought he was truly mad, like when he jetted off to the Middle East and came back with a computer system which we all joked was probably from Mossad, the Israeli intelligence service, that was designed to test an individual's ability to perform under high levels of stress and pressure. It all sounded very impressive, but when Clive appeared with this new state-of-the-art computer it was just a game with a joystick – the sort of thing they have in arcades all around the country. Clive urged us to take it all very seriously. But it was plain daft and even he realised that by the end so it didn't last long. The thing with Clive was that he always thought that things were worth trying if there was any chance of them making just the smallest of difference to the team.

Clive spent years taking away every single obstacle in front of us, and making it as easy as possible for us to do our best. He expected a lot of us, but he gave a lot in return. If you are to have any chance of being the best that you can, you need to believe that the people around you have your best interests at heart, and are working hard to help you to become the best you can. When Clive Woodward appeared, and brought attacking coaches, defensive coaches, nutritional experts and all manner of other staff with him, we could see how seriously he was taking us. Even though we seemed to have sunk to a standard well below that of the southern hemisphere sides, Clive made us believe that we could bounce back and become the best side in the world.

Away from the England team, at the beginning of 1999, things started changing at Gloucester when Richard Hill left the club and Philippe Saint-André came in as coach. When Philippe first turned up at Gloucester he could speak hardly any English. I remember his brother coming along as well and he used to help translate and explain. Philippe was obviously a legend of the game, so we all knew we could learn a great deal from him. I wasn't sure how much I'd benefit, with him being the consummate back and me being a big lump of a forward, but I soon learnt that he loved props. When he'd played in France, he'd worked closely with the front-row players and realised how important they were. When he came to Gloucester he spent a lot of time talking to me in his peculiar Franglais, asking about the scrum, the breakdowns and what the front rows had been doing. He was passionate, interested and determined to make the transition from brilliant player to brilliant coach.

In every way he was learning on the job, but he was good. He kept things simple and straightforward and kept saying, 'Go forward, be aggressive. We need good scrums and good lineouts.' If that was his philosophy, then it suited me. As time went on, there were increasing numbers of French players and French staff arriving at Gloucester. It amounted to sixteen French players there at one point, along with a French physio. I think, on balance, that was too many, too much of a change, but Philippe was just filling the club with people whom he knew to be good. They were French because the people he'd worked with before had been French, so I completely understood why he did it. He was a good guy and encouraged strong bonds between the forwards and the backs which helped the club immensely.

I managed to pick up a neck injury at this time. It was nothing very serious, certainly nothing as serious as the injuries that I would go on to have later in my career. I had damaged the fascia area and needed a few weeks out to recover from it. While I was recuperating, England played the Netherlands in a World Cup qualifier, winning 110-0. It was nice to see the boys on the winning end of a cricket score for a change. The match was the first time in which Martin Johnson captained England. He'd led the Lions very successfully in 1997, but this was the first time he'd led an England outfit. He'd stepped into the captain's shoes after Lawrence Dallaglio was caught in a *News of the World* sting and lost the captaincy.

The whole episode with Lawrence was a horrible shock. He's a good captain, a good player and a good man and it was horrible to see him put through the wringer like that. He made a silly mistake and said some daft things to a journalist because he thought she was an executive from a sponsorship company. These were the days when the sport had just gone professional, Lawrence probably hadn't dealt with a sponsor in negotiations like that before, he said some daft things in order to try and impress the fake sponsor, but that's all. I think he paid a high price for his misjudgement.

A week after the game against the Netherlands, England played Italy and won, albeit narrowly, meaning they had qualified for the 1999 World Cup. Then they prepared themselves to face Australia in November. This was obviously something of a grudge match after what had happened on tour, but this time they had a full England team out and they fared much better, losing narrowly 11–12. A week later I watched them play South Africa in another grudge match. This time England emerged with a 13–7 victory and the team's win ended the Springboks' amazing run of seventeen Test victories. While England moved things up a gear, I carried on working hard on my rehab, determined to get myself back in the team in time for the World Cup.

The build-up to the 1999 World Cup was like nothing I had ever known before. It was classic Clive Woodward: no stone was left unturned, no effort was spared. I'll be honest, at the time I don't think I realised just what a big deal World Cup tournaments were. Because the competition was based largely in England and Wales, it didn't feel like we were preparing for a big dramatic event. We knew we'd be staying at the Petersham, the hotel in Richmond where we always stayed, and would be training at the Bank of England ground, where we often trained. As I thought about the World Cup approaching, I suppose I thought about it more as an extended Five Nations competition than a major world tournament.

That view changed a little bit when I heard about the preparation that would be undertaken. We were told by Clive that this was the first World Cup of the professional era and that all the teams we faced would be bigger, fitter and stronger than at any previous tournament, so to that end we were forced to train very hard, with a new and terrifyingly professional guy called Dave Reddin. He was a complete nightmare! Beasting us with these fitness drills, tests and new expectations, he pushed us harder, fitness wise, than anyone had pushed us before, but boy did we need it. Reddin was a great guy and very talented, he knew his world completely. I'd be lying if I said that he was popular amongst the front-row players, though ... especially front-row players like me who've smoked roll-ups since they were 14.

One of the first things we did, in preparation for the tournament, was to go on a trip down to the Royal Marines Commando Training Centre in Lympstone, Devon. Clive had been eager for us to do this because he thought that if we were ever going to operate in an elite culture we had to understand exactly what an elite squad looked like. We arrived in Lympstone and waited in the officers' mess for the four-day training programme to start. None of us had a clue what to expect.

Lieutenant Nathan Martin was introduced to us as the man who would be in charge for the next four days, and he explained that we would be treated like Royal Marines. This was both an exciting prospect and a terrifying one. He said that we would be doing a series of military train-ing operations to test our leadership skills, decision-making under pressure, communication and teamwork skills. It all sounded fine. All I was worried about was whether they'd make me yomp. I'm not bloody built for yomping, and I was slightly concerned that we would end up having to go yomping across the countryside for days on end.

The next morning, bright and early (everything in the Marines seems to involve early mornings, as I was soon to discover), we assembled and were put into five teams. I was in Team 3 with Martin Johnson, Richard Hill, Victor Ubogu, Darren Garforth, Phil Greening and Martin Corry. A specialist mountain leader training instructor was put with each group and we were told that an enemy terrorist organisation had established themselves in a nearby stronghold and we had to find them. We were told that each team would be marked on points, and there would be a competition between teams to see which squad performed the best.

The Marines have a saying that even the best-laid plans go wrong. They call it 'dislocated expectations' – and much of their training is about experiencing the unexpected, in order to learn to cope with it. Since this is exactly what happens on a rugby pitch, I could see why Clive was so keen for us to go through this.

It was an amusing moment when we were all taken over to the stores depot to be kitted out in basic military field equipment. Royal Marines are generally not big men, they are average size and very thin, so finding gear to fit me was a huge challenge. My thighs were the same size as a normal Marine's waist. Over the next four days I discovered that it's hard to do the Royal Marines training when you are built like a tank. I remember, at one point, there were all these tunnels to go through, and I could barely fit through them normally, let alone when racing at high speed, in kit and carrying weapons.

And it wasn't just the bigger guys who had trouble – it was difficult if you were small, too. Poor Richard Cockerill discovered this when we were doing one exercise and you had to jump into four or five feet of water, carrying weapons and not getting them wet. Poor Cockerill jumped in and found the water was over his head. That wasn't enough to stop him, though. He just kept walking, holding his box (that's what we used to simulate a weapon) above his head without getting it wet at any stage. He had to jump up for air every so often, but he kept on going. Big respect!

There were loads of things that we were asked to do during those four days, many of which were completely new to us, like abseiling and going on the high wire. I was in the same group as Jerry Guscott, Austin Healey, Lawrence and Johno at one stage. Many of the guys were really fit and experienced and took to everything straight away; then there was me, this silly Billy Farmer who had never done anything like this before but was too scared to say he hadn't, so pretended he knew what he was doing. I just kept quiet and conformed to peer pressure. I did what was expected of me, and didn't tell anyone how concerned or worried I was.

In the end, I adapted to the whole thing by creating my own job ... I put myself in charge of anything that needed carrying. I told them 'Give it to the donkey' whenever there was any carting of stuff around the place to be done. We carried these electric poles across Dartmoor at one point, and we were supposed to debate who carried them and for how long. I just said, 'Give them here, I'll carry them,' and I carried them all the way. I'm good at doing jobs like that. I get my head down and plough on.

At one point when I was carrying the poles, it was quite funny because I was standing holding the front of the pole and Jerry Guscott was stuck holding the back of it.

We were walking along and Jerry was in this little dream world of his and not concentrating on where he was going at all. I stepped into a bog and disappeared down into the water, but Jerry wasn't watching what was happening, so instead of stopping and taking more of the weight of the pole to help me get out of my mess, he kept going, forging on with the pole, until the pole pushed me flat on my face in the water. I couldn't move, I thought I was going to drown, then I felt this big hand just lift me up out of the water so I could breathe again. I looked up and it was Johno. Just the guy you want at your shoulder when you're face down in water and about to be drowned.

We joined in with all sorts of exercises, including a simulated helicopter crash in which we were strapped into a life-size fuselage and dropped into a pool of water. Then we were assessed on how quickly and calmly we could escape as a team through a small hatch. After that we were flown by Sea King helicopter to a disused quarry on Dartmoor where there were more physical and mental challenges awaiting us, involving rope work, problem-solving, and a commando slide off a cliff face several hundred feet down to the bottom of a quarry.

Throughout our time on Dartmoor, plans kept chang-ing and expectations were challenged. We had to stay on our toes the whole time and react to events as they unfolded. In one emergency exercise we had to descend into the hold of a ship to repair a breach in the hull below the waterline, while cold seawater was flooding into the compartment as we carried out the exercise. We had to complete the job by each in turn holding our breath and plunging beneath the surface. It was one of the hardest things I've had to do.

We were really looking forward to getting back to the training centre and enjoying a nice hot meal and a comfortable bed on the last day, but of course, since it was the Marines, that was never going to happen. In a final twist, we were told that the helicopter would land 10 miles from the base and we would have to yomp all the way home with 60lb of gear on our backs in the final test of endurance.

The Marines were incredible, and the experience was priceless. When we left, there was a final speech in which we were told that we had experienced as near as possible a simulation of an operational mission in which briefings changed on an hourly basis. The Marines said that we might find some similarities with rugby, but emphasised that one mistake by a team-mate in war could cost you your life. They talked of the importance of good team-mates, and how you have to be able to look around at your fellow Marines and know that you would go into battle with them at your side. Would I go into battle with my team-mates? I'm pleased to say that in the England team I played for, I would go into battle with every one of them every time. Bring on the World Cup.

There was some good news at Gloucester at the end of the season as we finished third in the table, and qualified for the Heineken Cup the following season. The Heineken Cup is the best thing you can be involved in as a club so we were thrilled to be in the competition, but it's also very hard. It's not a quick jaunt at the end of the Premiership; you're playing the best club sides in Europe, and that's on top of the league fixtures. Meeting Toulouse and Cardiff is a big deal for any club and we knew we'd have to be firing to beat them. Having said that, we were all thrilled to be in the competition. Gloucester's a club with great ambition, and the Cup games were everything we'd worked towards. The idea of Cardiff coming to town with their fans and players was truly exciting. I knew that our fans would relish the chance to see even more great rugby, in a big Cup competition.

CHAPTER NINE:

THE 1999 WORLD CUP

It was the last year of the Millennium, and the first professional World Cup, and I was in the England squad and free of injury. My international rugby career was back on track. What a relief. Back in 1999 I had no idea quite what a big part injuries would end up playing in my career. I thought the neck injury was a one-off. What I realise now is that injuries are very much part and parcel of every international rugby player's life, and the ability to come back from them – mentally as well as physically – is a key part of having a successful career as a rugby player. My first match back after hurting my neck was against the United States at Twickenham in August, and I really wanted to show Clive that I was fully fit and raring to go.

We beat the USA 106–8 in what was a very one-sided match, then went on to play a second warm-up game a week later against Canada. The second match gave us another victory, this time by 36–11. We were ready for the World Cup, or so we thought ...

We moved into our regular hotel, the Petersham in Richmond, and played our first pool match on 2 October against Italy. It was a relatively easy start for us, but Italy were something of an unknown quantity back then. They weren't part of the Six Nations so we weren't as used to playing them. Despite that, we managed to come away with a 67–7 victory, playing some pretty good rugby and scoring eight tries in the process. The match belonged to Jonny Wilkinson who added 32 of the points, setting a new England record for most points in a Test, and filling us with hope about how his game would progress through the rest of the tournament.

The second game of the World Cup was the one that we were most eager to win. It was against the All Blacks, and winning it would mean topping our pool, and thus having a much easier route through the rest of the tournament. We went into the match feeling very confident because we now had a string of victories behind us, and had the benefit of home advantage. But we just didn't play well. In the first twenty minutes alone we missed several scoring opportunities, and you could feel that we were losing momentum. Things just weren't working for us. We lost 30–16, which was horribly disappointing because we knew it was a key game and the one match we desperately wanted to win. You could argue that that match lost us the World Cup because New Zealand topped our group and went on a fast track to the knock-out stages while we were forced to play an extra game before the quarter-final.

The feeling of frustration, of anger and disappointment, has never left me. It was an experience which left a very bitter taste in the mouths of everyone who went through it, and there's no doubt we vowed never to go through it again. We knew just how much had been lost when we were defeated by New Zealand. It wasn't just one match, it was as if our whole tournament was shattered in that moment. That sometimes happens in World Cups – even though the competition's a month long, there can be one hugely significant match buried in there that you need to win in order to do well.

The following week we beat Tonga 110–10, and the Tongans said they had felt like they were playing a team with something to prove. To be honest, they were right. We were all pissed off after the All Blacks game, and they got the full backlash. Even though we beat Tonga comfortably we emerged from it with lots of bumps and bruises and some more serious injuries in the team. The southern hemisphere sides are always tough to play, always very physical. We had to play two of them in a row, as we went on to play Fiji, winning 45–24. Again, the trouble was that we lost a lot of players through injury. Sometimes it's hard to play the smaller nations because they are desperate to beat England and make their World Cup a success story, so you can sometimes suffer more injuries in the smaller games against the lesser nations than playing against the big guns. So even though we had won both matches we had just three days to prepare and travel to Paris where we would meet a well-rested and determined South African side in the quarter-final.

South Africa had had nine days' rest before the match (they didn't have to play an additional play-off game which we'd had to because we lost to New Zealand and thus came second in the group). We went to Paris for the quarter-final having played two tough Pacific Island sides one after the other. Then we came up against the phenomenal drop-kicking of South African fly-half Jannie de Beer. He scored his points with five drop goals in a row in the space of thirty-one minutes in the second half, and the game was all over. His effort took South Africa to the semi-final at Twickenham, and left us licking our wounds and preparing for a trip back to England. It was crushing for all of us. We'd expected so much and been so full of hope – to have it dashed like that was almost unbearable.

It turned out later that Nick Mallett, the South Africa coach, had studied England's game carefully and came to the conclusion that a kicking game would be a sound counter to our more fluid game. That way the South Africans could reduce the threat of our back row. Our defence was good, so South Africa would just kick it over the top. I can see now that was a great game plan and shows what a good coach Mallett is. Back then I just felt like kicking the walls down.

Once you're out of a tournament, that's it. There's no messing around and hanging on to see how everyone else does. There was a players' reception the night of the game but I just don't remember anything about it – I was almost numb and just wanted to be out of there. The next morning we left Paris, feeling defeated in every sense of the word. The train ride back to London was sheer bloody agony. We were physically and mentally exhausted. It's so horrible going home after you've done badly in a tournament, and there's no question that losing in the quarter-final counted as having done very badly. The previous World Cup England had made it to the semi-finals, and in 1991 they'd made it to the final. Here we were, after more money had been spent on us than in any previous tournament, having done far worse than expected.

While the World Cup continued without us, we all went back to our homes and families and thought about what could have been. It was very strange to go from living so close to a group of guys, training with them, eating with them, playing with them under the most stressful circumstances for months, then going home and not seeing them again. It felt as if we couldn't get any lower. What we didn't realise at the time was that we wouldn't get any lower; we would use the defeat and the feelings from the Tour from Hell to motivate us to move upwards. It's all credit to Clive that we never felt like a bad group of players after we'd been knocked out of the World Cup, we felt like a group of players who were still to reach our potential. Clive was very insistent that this was just the start, and that we were to remember the pain we were feeling and use that to push us to work harder.

Losing in the World Cup, whilst horribly disappointing, didn't cripple me or make me feel dreadful. It made me feel frustrated and determined to do better next time, but not totally down and out. I always feel that if I work hard, do the right thing, and try to ignore what the papers say when things are going brilliantly or badly, I'll be OK. Things change so quickly in international sport that you can't listen when people are telling you that you are going to be a great rugby player or people are telling you that England are never going to win a thing, because you don't know either way. You might get injured the week after a great performance and never play again. No one knows what the future holds, and to put too much pressure on yourself to excel at sport will send you nuts. You have to have a balance in life.

The great thing for the England team was that while the articles were appearing, saying how useless we were and writing off all our chances of achieving anything, ever, we were busy building for the future and turning ourselves into a team that would never lose like that again. Clive brought in a new regime, a new approach to training, supplements, conditioning, and a complete change of mentality over the years that followed, and I'm sure the defeat in the World Cup was what prompted the changes. I said before how important I think the ability to cope with defeat is, and Clive used that defeat to launch us into the future.

We'd learnt that we weren't good enough and we needed to change that. We wanted to be the best, and never again to lose like we had done. I would say that the defeat in the 1999 World Cup quarter-final drew a line in the sand and things changed. Of course there would be more defeats to come, but none as grinding as that one. Clive was keener than ever to tell us that the England team needed to be more professional, like the Marines we'd trained with who were perfect physical specimens but who also worked brilliantly as a team. The roots of what would blossom into a World Cup victory in 2003 began to grow in those painful days after we had been knocked out of the 1999 World Cup.

CHAPTER TEN:

MAKING A STAND

It was after the untimely exit from the 1999 World Cup that Clive began introducing change after change to give us every possible advantage. There were lots of little things introduced, like us changing our shirts at half-time. We thought he'd gone bonkers when he first suggested it, and most of us were against it because there's not enough time to mess about with changing shirts halfway through a match, but he persuaded us to try. The statisticians had discovered that we played very well in the first ten minutes of any game, so he wanted us to try and replicate that at the beginning of the second half with a shirt change. It was only a little thing, and on its own it probably wouldn't have made a blind bit of difference to anything, but with all the other little improvements that Clive was making you felt they were starting to make a difference to how we felt as a team, and the way other countries looked at us.

Working with England under Clive Woodward was something of a revelation. He brought in so many new ideas and challenged so many of the old ones that it was sometimes difficult to keep up. When I first started at Gloucester, I'd been impressed that they had a video in the clubhouse which we could use to see how we had performed in the games. Now there was talk of ProZone following our every move on the pitch to see how fast we ran, where we ran to, and where we placed ourselves on the pitch.

But the great thing about Clive was that even though he collected lots of information and analysed it in detail, he didn't overwhelm us with feedback. You have to limit the amount of information you act on as a rugby player or you'll run around in circles on the pitch as you try to think of everything. You can't overload your brain. The coaches with England would discuss lots of information and give you top line feedback, then you, as a player, needed to filter that in order to make sure that you concentrated on the most important things. The ability to filter, focus and concentrate on what will affect you and improve your game is key to being successful as a player. It's one of the key skills that you have to develop and you can only learn it through experience.

When I first started out as a rugby player I wanted to know everything that was happening on the pitch. I felt it was important to have it very clearly in my head what everyone was going to be doing and what all the moves were. I now know that there's no need for me to know all the backs' moves. I just need to have an idea of what they're doing out there so I understand what they are going to try and do next, and what the implications are for me. I certainly don't have to know all the backs' moves inside out. If I know whether they're going to drift and, if so, where to, and what I need to do at breakdowns to help facilitate what the backs want to do, that's enough. I don't have to know Will Greenwood's running lines or Jonny Wilkinson's positioning. That takes experience and confidence, and that's what everyone in the England team was building up at this stage. Our ability to make real-time decisions on the pitch, even in what we called 'the fog of war', was crucial, and all these matches we were playing, even the ones we were losing (especially the ones we were losing), were teaching us how to do it.

We played the first game of the new Six Nations Championships – the first ever Six Nations (Italy joined the Five Nations after the World Cup) – and beat Ireland 50–18. It was during the next game, against France, that we changed our shirts at half-time for the first time. We played France at the Stade de France, which was never an easy place to play, and beating them 15–9 was a huge victory for us. Our shirt changing worked well too, and what's interesting is that other teams soon started copying us. When was the last time that happened? Other teams copying England's lead? The winds of change were beginning to blow.

We played Wales and won 46–12 at Twickenham, then I didn't play in the match against Italy which we won 59–12, but I was back in the side for the final match of the championships, against Scotland at Murrayfield. Only they stood between us and a Grand Slam. It seemed inconceivable that they would beat us. Many people talked ominously of the time in 1990 when England were definitely going to beat Scotland to win the Grand Slam but stumbled at the final fence. Ten years on, and Scotland denied us the Grand Slam once again. We lost 19–13 and it felt like such a setback after we'd beaten France in Paris. It was a dismal day, and there were mutterings from people that this new England team couldn't finish properly and didn't have the killer instinct to wrap up victories when it really mattered. I never thought that was very fair, and I resented the accusations that we should try harder and give more. We were giving everything. Other teams knew about the hard work being done by the England team, and were determined to beat us, to knock us down. We were the side that everyone wanted to beat, and while that was good training for the World Cup it was making life difficult in the short term.

At Gloucester we made it to the last four of the Heineken Cup after beating Cardiff in the quarter-final. That was an amazing achievement and a great occasion for the club as thousands of Cardiff supporters streamed into town. The match was great as well. Pete Rogers was playing for Cardiff and I'd come up against him numerous times when he was playing for Wales. He always used to come round the side of the scrum and nick the ball, so I was determined he wasn't going to get away with it in the club game. I'm pleased to report that I managed to stop him. We had the best of the scrums and we won the match. The supporters from both sides were amazing and it was a hell of an occasion. We lost to Leicester to stop us from getting to the final, but it had been a tight game that had gone right down to the wire, so we exited the Heineken Cup with our heads held high.

My season finished badly when I managed to get injured when playing for Gloucester (a shoulder injury), which had the effect of keeping me out of the 2000 South Africa tour, so I had to sit back and watch as England lost the first Test 18–13, then stunned the world by winning the second Test 27–22.

That autumn we played Australia at Twickenham and beat them. It was a huge match for us because it was one in which we psychologically broke Australia, which is a very hard thing to do. They are an extraordinarily confident team, with piles of mental strength, but we beat them 22–19 without even playing at our best and felt that we had got the better of them. For the first time, I think they ran onto the field thinking that we were a good side. This was a huge stepping stone on our journey to becoming the best team in the world. The next match we were due to play was against Argentina, but before we took the field to play them we had the small matter of a long-running negotiation with the RFU to sort out.

We'd started to feel fed up with the Rugby Football Union for a while. The sport was fully professional now, but it seemed that the players weren't really benefiting from its new status. We always felt as if we didn't have much of a voice, and as individuals we didn't. If one of us had started to complain about the way things were, the way we were being treated or the money we were earning, no one would have listened and it would have been easy to drop him from the side and play someone else, but collectively – as Team England – we definitely had a voice. We needed to stand together and challenge the Rugby Football Union. The players' representatives were

Martin Johnson, Lawrence Dallaglio and Matt Dawson, and they would represent us all. They had spoken to the RFU before the Australia game about the fact that we felt that too high a percentage of our match fees was linked to winning. We thought that most of our match fee should be just that – a match fee – with a small proportion of it held back as a win bonus. This seemed to be fair. It seemed especially key to us because at this time we were being asked to give away our image rights by the RFU which meant that they could license our images for advertisers and sponsors however they wanted to, so we could be used to promote anything with no say in the matter and for no payment. If they were going to do that, then it seemed only fair that they should give in to one of our requests that we be paid a fee rather than a win bonus.

The whole issue was causing lots of tension, and for us it wasn't about the money (we were talking about relatively small figures in any case – we were trying to convince them that we were worth £4,000 per man no matter what the result, whereas the union's final offer was a £3,500 match fee), it was about the principle of them wanting to take, take, take all the time and not give anything back in return. It was simply unfair. This wasn't about us jeopardising our future as England rugby players for the sake of an extra guaranteed £500 per man per game. There was a principle at stake, and it was worth fighting for.

The new professionalism needed to be worked out, and the two sides at loggerheads here – the RFU and us in the England team – were having our first major battle over where the real power lay as much as anything else. The RFU felt that they had all the power because we were so keen to play for England and were unlikely to do anything to compromise that, but when the players were all together as a group, and of the same mind, we did have considerable power. They couldn't drop us all ... could they? I hoped not.

The RFU said that they wouldn't budge from their £3,500 match fee deal. We said we weren't happy, now what should we do? Refuse to play? March on Twickenham and start kicking the place apart? Probably not a good idea. In the end, it seemed that our options were to strike, something that nobody wanted to do, or refuse to get involved in any commercial activities. We decided that this latter option was the right thing. It meant we wouldn't attend pre-match sponsors' dinners, and we would turn our sponsored clothing inside out so that the sponsors' logos wouldn't be seen by TV cameras. None of us felt comfortable about doing this, because we would be punishing the sponsors and this was not their fault, but we didn't know what else to do. We told the RFU ahead of the Australia fixture what our plans were, and Clive stepped in to persuade us to delay our action until after the Australia game. We agreed to this, and in return Clive said he would get the RFU President Budge Rogers to a meeting on the Monday after the Australia game to discuss this further. After the Australia game, Budge duly came along, but the meeting got us nowhere. The RFU's stance remained the same. We were all aware that the RFU expected us to back down, but we knew that we couldn't, or we'd be letting down generations of future players. We had to show that when the players got together to make a stand they meant business. Suddenly it had gone from small-time plans to turn our T-shirts inside out to all-out war. We had come to the point where we needed to take some action.

We all went to a meeting in Johno's room where we discussed everything and voted on whether we should strike – something that none of us wanted to do, but we now felt we had no choice. Johno, Lawrence Dallaglio and Matt Dawson, the guys heading up the team, made it clear what the repercussions of what we were doing would be. I have to be honest, I was quite prepared to strike, I thought it was the most sensible option. I certainly never felt bullied into striking by the others. It was very much a case of us being offered the chance to do so, and of voting on it. It was a very fair vote, very democratic. I wanted what was best for everyone. I wanted what was best for the team in the long term as well as for the team of guys around me on that day. The problems in the England set-up needed to be sorted out once and for all, so it was clear what the deal was. Everything needed to be more transparent. There were so many things that weren't professionally run. We felt that we were doing our side of things as professional players, training and working hard, but the RFU weren't adhering to their side of the bargain. Perhaps our strike would help change their minds.

Clive was furious when he found out what we were planning to do, of course, and I do understand why he reacted so strongly to the news, because he felt that he and the coaches were putting in a colossal amount of work to create a fabulous environment in which we as players could prosper. I guess he thought, to some extent, that we were throwing this back in his face. But from our point of view we had no choice. Rugby was still relatively new into professionalism and was finding its feet, and we needed to make sure that our views were taken into the equation during this process.

As players we felt that was the very last consideration of everyone at the Rugby Football Union, and we sensed that there was a residual feeling that we should be very grateful to be selected to play for England in the first place and just get on with it, regardless of the money or expectations of us. Not a day went by when I didn't feel grateful for the opportunity to play for England, but that wasn't the point. Many at the RFU didn't seem to have fully embraced the idea of professionalism and their feeling was that we shouldn't be worrying about money and just be getting on with playing. Now I'm someone who's never been motivated by money, but the thing is that playing rugby at international level is very hard, it demands every ounce of you, and we didn't want to go into matches feeling slighted and put out. It was important that we got together and did something to redress what we thought was an unfairness. And, whichever way you look at it, it isn't fair for the RFU to charge huge amounts of money to sponsors, vast amounts for tickets, and sell TV rights for billions, use that money to pay lots of officials of the game very well, and then to balk at the players' requests for reasonable payments. You're either amateur or professional, and the sport was now professional.

Even at the time we knew that what we were doing wasn't just about us, this particular group of players in this moment in this match. This was about asserting the players' rights to be taken seriously in the new professional game. We needed to make sure that future players would not be treated like this. So we went on strike.

It provoked thousands of headlines and was quite a serious deal for the younger players in the squad, many of whom were terrified that their careers were over. I remember that Chris Fortey was invited down to England training for the first time, and when he arrived he discovered it was the first day of the strike. He couldn't believe it. Having wanted to play for England all his life, he found himself on strike before he'd even started training. You've got to feel sorry for guys put in that situation.

For all that, we had to strike to draw a line in the sand separating the old amateur game from the new professional one. There had to be a change in the way things were being done. In the end the result of the ballot had been almost unanimous, with just one or two absentees, both senior players, so it wasn't as if half the players were happy and half weren't. The vast majority of the players were so unhappy that they were willing to strike.

Poor Johno had the task of going to tell the RFU that we were refusing to play Argentina that weekend. Christ, I wouldn't have wanted to be in his shoes when he told Clive. Sure enough, Clive reacted with fury and told us that if we were on strike and not preparing for the match, then we should leave the team hotel. We packed up and left while the RFU hurriedly called a press conference to get their point of view across to the media. It was a really strange time because we were portrayed as these money-grabbers, but it wasn't like that at all. I don't think there was anyone in that England team who you could honestly describe as being money-grabbing.

That night we all went to the Café Royal for a fundraising event for Alastair Hignell, who had recently been diagnosed with multiple sclerosis. We'd said we'd go, and we didn't want to let people down, especially Alastair, so we went despite everything that was going on. It was a difficult evening because the place was full of press who obviously wanted to know what the latest development was. They asked me and I just shrugged. I had no idea, but with guys like Martin Johnson, Lawrence Dallaglio and Matt Dawson in charge, I felt as if the right decision would be made.

The next day we managed to reach a settlement that was somewhere between the two positions, and we agreed to play the game. It was a huge relief.

One thing that the whole strike did for me was to reaffirm in my own mind exactly how much rugby means to me, and why I play it. Of course, like everyone else in the England team, I don't play the sport for money, I play it because I love it … but the strike was all about the players coming together and acting as one, and I approved of that, as I approve of it on the pitch.

During the strike we'd all stuck together and been there for one another. There's something about playing with people you trust and admire that makes rugby special for me; you look into their eyes and they know you have that bond with them that is essential for the team to work. You don't have to tell people how great you think they are and you don't have to thank people for what they do for you on the pitch ... it is all much more subtle, and much deeper than that. Every time someone helps you on a rugby field it just adds to the respect you have for them, and tightens the bond on the field.

I knew by this stage of my career just what sacrifices were needed to make it to the top of English rugby. While professionalism had brought money into the game, it had also upped the pressure and expectations of the players. There was the training, and the big things like going away and not seeing your family as much as you want to, as well as the small things like not eating that pizza because you knew it wasn't good for you. Sacrifice is what it takes to get to the top. Sacrifice is important because it is part of this will to win, whatever it takes, to make you successful.

England at this time was full of men who would do that. You can look back now and cast your mind over the faces in that squad ... they were men willing to do whatever it took to win. We got through the whole strike crisis, and emerged a more unified squad at the end of it.

CHAPTER ELEVEN:

LIONS ROAR

Being selected to play for the Lions was out of this world. I know that's a terrible cliché but I can't think of any other way of describing the experience. The truth is that I never dreamt of playing for England, let alone running out for the British and Irish Lions. To me, selection for the Lions represents the greatest achievement in rugby so it was an unbelievably special occasion when I found out I'd be playing for them in Australia in the summer of 2001. I remember ringing Mum and she didn't know what to say. Everything had come so bloody quickly ... one minute I was at Redruth, then I was at Gloucester and within a couple of years I was in the England team, playing in a World Cup, and now the Lions. 'What's next?' she asked. But as far as I was concerned this was it, the highest honour in all of rugby.

I didn't have much experience as an international player, so I was quite nervous turning up to meet the other guys and seeing all the legends of the game standing there, but I soon learnt the most important thing about the Lions is that it's new for everyone, and we're all nervous when we first arrive. No one knows what it'll be like with new coaches and new playing partners. Everyone's out of their comfort zone and thrown together; and that's one of the many things that's great about it. Lions tours are a real leveller; it doesn't matter what you've achieved all season, now you have to achieve it all again. This time you've got players you've been fighting against all season in the team with you. Quite an odd concept when you think about it. Lions tours also break down all barriers since you have to make great friends and form playing partnerships with people you've never known much about before. And you have to do it quickly.

There'd been a certain amount of talk before the tour that it was wrong that Graham Henry was coaching the Lions because he's a New Zealander. There was a feeling that it should be a British coach who was handed the honour of the greatest coaching job in Britain. I suppose it would have been easier for me if Clive Woodward had been the coach of the tour as many thought he should have been, because then I would have known what to expect from the tour, but it was also good to be forced out of my comfort zone, and to be made to work with other coaches. The more people you work with, and the more people you can learn off, the better for you as a player.

In the event, I met Graham Henry and got on with him straight away. I take people as I find them and he was decent to me from the start. He was always well mannered. I never had any problems with him at all despite what might have been written in the press about the players falling out with him on tour.

I enjoyed his take on the way he wanted us to play the game (which was quite detailed and complex) and we tried very hard to embrace his feelings on the game. We all worked our guts out and I think we went a long way to try and play rugby as he believed it should be played, but it's difficult on Lions tours to totally change your game and adapt to new formations, new strategies, new calls and a new philosophy. We knew that Australia would have a settled team of players who'd spent a lot of time working together, whereas the Lions were coming together for the first time to take them on in their own backyard.

We had to spend a while learning what the new game plan was and how the other players played. That's what makes it hard, but that's also what makes a Lions tour a fantastic rugby experience, travelling across the country playing lots of teams with a group of players that you're quickly getting to know. We had guys like Rob Henderson, Brian O'Driscoll, Dai Young, Keith Wood ... it was a hell of an experience.

We all got together at Tylney Hall, a magnificent hotel outside London – thirty-seven of us from different backgrounds, getting to know one another as quickly as possible during the week. We did all sorts of daft team-building exercises that involved playing tambourines and drums and stuff like that. The management were hoping that we'd lose our inhibitions and bond as a team if we all stepped out of our comfort zones a bit and made fools of ourselves. I'm not normally big on all that corporate team-building nonsense, but I decided to give it a go, and bang my tambourine along with everyone else.

With all the work we were doing, it was great to see relationships growing amongst the guys on the team, and a sense of team building. We knew this would develop naturally as the tour went on but appreciated that Graham wanted to move that process on as quickly as possible and get us working together as a team before even heading for Australia. We were encouraged to talk about difficult things that happened to us, and to open up about private fears and concerns. Again, I thought it was a bit odd at first, but the truth is that you saw people being vulnerable and it did make you realise that however many caps a guy's got, and however big and strong he may be, he's human, just like the rest of us.

We trained a great deal as well, at the army's training centre, near Aldershot. We worked hard in those sessions, and after a knackering season some people were finding it too much. There were voices raised in complaint as players thought they'd be exhausted before we even made it to the first Test. I personally thought it was important that we worked together on the pitch as much as possible, so I did understand why there was a real interest in getting us onto the training field together as much as possible. Phil Larder, the rugby league coach, was in charge of defence and it was his responsibility to organise us as a unit. Phil did the same thing for England under Clive Woodward but it's much harder with the Lions. With England we had a load of time to play together and build up a fantastically well-organised defence. If Phil was to have any chance of replicating that with the Lions, he needed to have lots of time with us all out on the field working on it. I realised why we had to train so hard, but I also understood why some of the players were becoming agitated because they were exhausted after a long season.

Things didn't change when we touched down in Australia. The training was hard and there was lots of it because Graham wanted us to play in a structured way with lots of phases of play. There was a lot to learn and a lot to get to grips with, and players were beginning to flag and blamed Graham for over-complicating things. I'll say straight away that I never felt like this myself, but I understood their concerns and I hated that there was disharmony in the ranks before we'd even played the first game. This wasn't what I'd expected to find on a Lions tour.

The first match was against Western Australia and we won handsomely, emerging with a 116–10 victory. The result was great, but we were starting to struggle with injuries. Phil Greening had hurt his knee and Mike Catt his calf. Simon Taylor, the Scotland No. 8, damaged his knee in the second half and was on his way home ... after one match. It seemed that the long, exhausting season was starting to catch up with many of the players, and we had a hell of a lot of injuries.

Next it was the Queensland President's XV who we smashed before flying to Brisbane to beat the Queensland Reds 42–8. But despite us winning well and scoring lots of tries, the Australian newspapers began their 'Lions are boring' campaign, accusing us of being dull to watch.

None of this bothered me, as I've said before, and I'm so used to it with England that it feels odd to tour Australia and not be called boring.

Our players were dropping at such a rate that we wondered who would be left standing by the time the first Test came along. Behind the scenes there continued to be some tense times, with Graham managing to upset some of the players with his team talk when he said, 'These people down here in the southern hemisphere doubt your skills. I know. I'm one of them.' I don't think he meant that in a literal way at all, it was just a daft little joke, but with a team of exhausted players who were becoming increasingly fed up, it was taken the wrong way, and I know that some people became a bit fed up with him. It also seemed to confirm many people's worries about having a foreign coach on tour. They felt that a British coach would never say anything like that to them.

The last game before the first Test arrived, against Waratahs, and with it came the traditional battering from the Wallabies coach, Rod Macqueen. Macqueen and Waratahs coach Bob Dwyer both started spouting all sorts of rubbish, saying that we were playing illegally in the scrum, the lineout, and even at the breakdown. Two grown men trying to convince the public that we were playing illegally when we were clearly not.

The match was incredible because of the great support we had from Lions fans. The stadium was packed with red shirts and the chants of 'Lions, Lions, Lions!' could be heard from the changing rooms as we prepared to run out onto the pitch. It's astonishing to be on the other side of the world, so far from home, and to see that level of support turning out for you. What I also found was that it was wonderful to be cheered and clapped by Scottish and Welsh and Irish supporters. Of course, I realise that when the Lions tour the fans support all the players in the team, but it was still a very pleasant surprise to me when I saw that happen for myself.

The downside of the game, and what it will be best remembered for afterwards, was Duncan McRae's assault on Ronan O'Gara. McRae had O'Gara pinned down on the ground and hit him several times in the face without O'Gara doing anything in response. When Ronan left the field he had blood streaming down his face and a horrible nasty gash underneath his eye. It's hard to imagine what provoked McRae to behave like that. There didn't seem to be any reason for it at all.

The referee sent off McRae and a few minutes later a small fight broke out between a few of us who were very unhappy about what had happened to Ronan. There's no place in rugby for violence like that. As a result of our mini-brawl I was sent off along with Danny Grewcock, and Brendan Cannon and Cameron Blades from the Waratahs walked too. It was just one of those silly incidents that happens in rugby sometimes. It shouldn't have happened but you can't just stand there when one of your team-mates gets smashed in the face. Of course, because the front rows were off, there was a ridiculous merry-go-round of substitute players coming on to try to keep the scrum going until we got back on, but we managed a 41–24 victory despite it all.

The injury jinx we seemed to be suffering from continued, with news that Dan Luger's fractured cheekbone from an earlier match would end his tour, as well as Will Greenwood going off with a serious ankle injury. Neil Back had an injured hand and Lawrence Dallaglio had taken a knock on his knee. There were a lot of players out, and the first Test was just around the corner.

There was much talk in the press about the whole team being divided and not getting on with Graham Henry. I don't think it was anything like as bad as people thought it was. The only division started to occur because of the resentment bubbling in those players who perceived they were mid-week players and as such felt like they would never have a chance of getting into the Test team.

I would discover, when I went on tour in 2009, that on some Lions tours you can keep the whole squad together with everyone feeling as if they have a shot at a Test place, but it would be fair to say that a lot of people didn't feel like that in 2001. It felt very much as if Graham had decided on the Test team and the mid-week team and they were training quite separately. There was one train-ing session for the Saturday side and one to prepare the Tuesday boys for their game, which was to be against the New South Wales Country Cockatoos.

But then Graham Henry changed things, and brought us all together and told the mid-week side that they would have to play as the Wallabies to try and test out the defence of the guys chosen for the Test 22. It felt like a snub to the mid-week guys, who now felt that they were not only a second-class team but they were being used to train the first team. Some of them talked of feel-ing like cannon fodder. I can see what the management were thinking of in focusing on the Test match; obviously it seemed daft to focus our attention on beating a little team called the Cockatoos when the tour would live or die depending on how we played in the Tests. The Tests were clearly the matches we needed to focus on. Perhaps Graham could have been less blunt and obvious about this, though, because he had a situation where half the squad was feeling disgruntled.

Things weren't helped when we had some terrible news. Anton Toia, the liaison officer supplied by the Australia Rugby Union to look after us, had a heart attack and died in the sea after a fishing trip with the other players. We all thought Anton was great, and I liked him very much. I suppose, in some ways, his death did put our little niggles into perspective; on the other hand it just brought everyone down even further and made us all feel quite miserable.

We went on to beat the Cockatoos 46–3 and all the focus shifted to the first Test, to be played at the Gabba. This first Test was always going to be a tough match. Lions tours are hard, and we were on the other side of the world about to play the World Champions. We were aware that thousands of people had spent a lot of money to travel over to watch the Lions and that seemed to add to the pressure even though we valued their support enormously.

On the day, as we ran out on the pitch, there were red shirts everywhere, people from all corners of the stadium shouting for the Lions, and you realise just how special this sport is. The game started well, with a try from Jason Robinson that was stunning. Jase has got such explosive pace, and he showed it in all its glory in this match. I can't think about that first Test now without recalling that incredible try. We had about 2 minutes and 45 seconds on the clock when Jason touched down to put us five points up, and the Lions supporters in the crowd went wild. It was a dream start. We scored again and at half-time the score was 12–3. By full-time we'd made it 29–13.

It was a wonderful feeling, and everything that had happened before the Test seemed to be forgotten. Then, shortly after the victory, we were all told about a column written by Matt Dawson criticising the way the tour was going. It had appeared on the morning of the Test and it was all that the journalists wanted to talk to any of us about. Matt had written the piece when he was pissed off. He didn't feel like he was getting a fair shot at the No. 9 shirt, because Rob Howley made it his own, and in a moment of madness had written a column for a newspaper. I didn't take it seriously at all. Matt is a good bloke, he's a great rugby player and a good friend, and we all make mistakes. If Matt had been as pissed off at training as he said he was in his column, he never showed it, as far as I can recall. He was always there at training, always giving it his all. That's what really matters – not what the guy writes in a newspaper column. I shrugged it off, told Matt not to worry, and I never thought about it again. We had won the first Test and now needed to win the next two. We could be part of history if we could make this back-to-back wins for the Lions.

There was never any chance of me getting too carried away with myself, though, or starting to think I was more important than I am, because there was always the family to bring me back down to earth. I phoned my father on the farm, just to let him know how things were, and he asked me when I was coming home. I told him I had a couple of bills to pay in Gloucester, and that I'd be down in Cornwall in three weeks. 'Brilliant,' he said. 'Just in time to help me with the silage.' So there it is. I've just played rugby for eleven months, and I'll be starting my holiday knee-deep in you know what. It's a wonderful world, isn't it?

I remember Donal Lenihan coming out to talk to us before the second Test in Melbourne and saying, 'The Lions have an incredibly long history and in all that time only once since the 1890s have they achieved back-to-back Test series wins, in 1971 and 1974 ...' It gave us a sense of just what an opportunity we had in this match, and how much credit we could bring to the Lions shirt.

Despite the rousing talk before kick-off, the second Test was disappointing. It was a night game, Melbourne is a fantastic place to play rugby and once again we had loads of support everywhere. But Australia had upped their game and they were a much more impressive side than they had been earlier. They beat us 35–14, which was a record defeat for the Lions against Australia. Worse still, Richard Hill and Rob Howley were both injured. It was quite a ridiculous situation when Rob Howley was injured because Austin Healey went down with a back injury before the final Test, meaning that we had lost two scrum-halves so only had Matt Dawson left with no cover for him. Someone spotted Andy Nicol, who was in Australia leading a supporters' tour party, and he was drafted out of the bar and into the squad in advance of the next match.

In the second Test, Australia had improved their scrummaging considerably. The Wallabies have a reputation as a great all-round side, but not as a great scrummaging unit, and quite honestly some of the scrummaging in Australia borders on pantomime. If I had to scrum like some of the Wallabies, I wouldn't bother. You long to say, 'Come on, let's see what you've got. This is a game of rugby, not a tea party.'

But the Wallaby front row we confronted in the second Test was good. They'd changed their personnel, done their homework and settled on a plan of action that worked well for them. There'd been a great deal of talk before the Tests about the weakness of the Australian front row, but you don't win World Cups and Tri-Nations titles without a proud pack of forwards, so I knew they'd be better than people were making them out to be. I have no doubt that the bad-mouthing fuelled them. I also think they drew strength from the presence of Michael Foley at hooker. I rated Foley. He was a good set-piece man, a hard nut, and he tightened up their act to great effect.

I knew that if we were to have any chance of winning the third Test we would have to deal with Foley. It seemed to me that this was one of the key things that we had to do before going into the final Test.

The Lions is so big that every emotion is extreme. When you win, as we did in Brisbane, you're the happiest bloke in the world. When things go badly, as they did in Melbourne, it hurts more than you can imagine. Rugby at this level is a personal challenge, and you beat yourself over the head about this or that aspect of your game. My tackle count in Melbourne was desperate; for the first time in many moons I failed to hit double figures. I spoke to Phil Larder and we talked about how I could have done things differently, and I knew it wouldn't happen again. Then there was the lineout, another basic phase in which we let ourselves down. I buggered it up on a couple of occasions, simply because someone changed the call and I either wasn't listening or couldn't hear because of the crowd noise.

You have a choice when things go badly in the match – you sulk, or you get it sorted. Before the third Test we put in a really good week's work on the fundamentals of forward play. We had our heart-to-heart sessions and we were honest with each other about where we'd gone wrong and what we needed to do better in the next Test. We talked about how the game represented a once-in-a-lifetime opportunity, an opportunity that was worthy of us throwing everything we had at it.

I knew that if we played to our potential and lost, it would be fine. I'd be the first to hold out my hand and congratulate the opposition, but if we messed it up again, all this would have been a pointless exercise. And that really would upset me.

For the final Test we stayed at the Manly Hotel, and before the game started we had another diary issue to deal with as news broke that Austin Healey had written a piece in the *Guardian* in which he had called Justin Harrison, the Australian second row, a 'plod', a 'plank' and an 'ape'. Again, it wasn't something that bothered me unduly. I thought he was daft to have written it, but I knew we couldn't let it affect us with the third Test just hours away.

We were playing the final Test at Stadium Australia and Jason Robinson once again got us off to a flying start with a try that gave us a 10–9 lead after early penalties. It felt like a finely balanced game, and one that we could win. In the second half Jonny Wilkinson went over to make it 20–16, before Australia came back. In the end we lost 29–23 in what was a hugely disappointing match because we knew we should have won the game.

There were lots of problems with that final Test; among them was the ridiculous situation with the lineout calls, where we kept the same calls as we'd used previously. Looking back now, that sounds daft. Australia were bound to be able to work out what we were up to. I remember being in a lineout and the Australian prop said when he heard a call, 'OK, that means they're going to throw it to the middle and move the ball back.' It's a bit disconcerting when you realise that the opposition knows your lineout calls better than you do. The other mistake we made was practising in open spaces. We did some of our practice moves in parks and places like that. The Australians are well known for their spying tactics, so I guess they just worked on finding out where we were training, so they could find out what we were planning to do in the lineouts. We should have been more careful.

After the end of the tour, and the disappointment of us losing the series, the fans were still in good spirit and good voice. There was singing and drinking at the bars along the seafront next to the players' hotel after the final Test. I remember that Rob Henderson was still out drinking in the same clothes he had been in all day. He told me he'd better go and get changed, but instead of going back to our hotel he walked round the corner into the nearest shop, where he bought a shirt and trousers and put the clothes he was wearing into the bin, and walked straight back into the bar and carried on drinking. He hadn't wanted to head all the way back to the hotel because he might miss precious drinking time!

When we came back from the Lions tour, we had the summer off before heading for Ireland to play the final game of the Six Nations Championship that had been delayed because of foot-and-mouth disease earlier in the year. So, exhausted from a Lions tour and not having played with England for months, we headed for Dublin in October. The England team had played some great rugby in the first four matches of the Six Nations and were favourites to beat Ireland to win the Grand Slam. The trouble was, delaying the match until October meant we were horribly unprepared, many of us had been on the Lions tour and we couldn't get any more time away from our clubs to train with England. So we had to go into the match without being ready for it at all.

In the end, I think Ireland played better than we did. Our lineout was a disaster in the first half and we made loads of errors around the pitch. They won 20–14, and once again we had come desperately close to winning a Grand Slam before losing it all in the final game. It was massively disappointing considering we had eleven victories on the run up to that point. It was very hard to take, especially since the newspapers were full of articles about how we didn't have that extra edge to win when it really mattered. We all knew that wasn't true, but it was hard to read it.

We had won every match leading up to that Ireland game, and many thought that we were invincible. There was a feeling that England couldn't be beaten. It teaches you a lesson to realise that you can always be beaten. You can't get lost in it and convince yourself that you can't lose. The nuts and bolts have to be tightened down, the detail has to be right. We simply weren't prepared for that match, and we lost. That's the way it should be. It didn't mean we were a terrible side; it meant we needed to take lessons on board and become a better side.

CHAPTER TWELVE:

CAPTAIN PHIL AND THE ARGENTINIANS

Clive Woodward was a forward-looking coach. His search for ways in which we could be ever more effective on the pitch led him to looking at all things to do with the England set-up. One conclusion was that the shirts we were wearing needed changing. He wanted to do away with the old baggy, heavy shirts, and introduce lightweight versions. Now I'm not sure that I was built for skin-tight Lycra. Props aren't. We're built for pushing, shoving, crashing and bashing, not posing around in the sort of material they use to make leotards.

Still, against the advice of every forward who ever lived, Clive produced these shirts that showed every rippling muscle or ounce of fat, depending on who you were. I suppose I was lucky in some ways, because we had to test lots of different options for the new shirt, and I remember at one stage there was Dan Luger in an all-in-one on the training pitch. An all-in-one? I'd have looked like an overweight extra from Abba. Luckily, the International Rugby Board declared that playing in an all-in-one was illegal because the laws stated that you had to have separate shorts and shirts. Thank the Lord. Can you imagine what an idiot I'd have looked in that get-up?

We wore the new shirts, and despite all our reservations they were great, especially for the backs who could run freely and slide through tackles. There was no spare material to grab onto, making our backs harder to tackle. Once we'd worn them a few times, the old shirts seemed daft – they'd get wet and incredibly heavy. Lots of new things seem odd when they first appear but once you start using them it seems absurd that you weren't trying them before. Like kicking tees ... why did we not have kicking tees before? Clive was good about introducing new things, even though people mocked and thought him barmy. He kept pushing the boundaries and urging us to do things differently.

Away from rugby, in 2002 I decided to move home, so I sold my place in exchange for a bigger house with a bit of land. I was pottering around inside the new house, sorting things out and working out where everything would go, when this girl turned up because her horses had been using the land when the previous owners were there. She'd come to collect them. I couldn't believe it when she arrived. I thought she was stunning. I gave her all my numbers and told her to call if she needed anything, but of course she never called and I thought I'd never see her again.

A few months after that, I spotted her in a nightclub in Gloucester. I knew I had to find the courage to go and talk to her in case I didn't bump into her again, so I went over and asked her whether she remembered me. I gave her my number again, this time written on a £10 note. I thought that was bound to impress her. Apparently she took it home and her Dad said, 'He's no good. The number should be written on a £20 note.'

Just for good measure I'd got her number as well, so the day after bumping into her I summoned up the courage to make the phone call to her. The phone rang and I felt so nervous, then one of those tinny automated voices said, 'This number is not recognised.' Damn. One of the numbers must be wrong. I tried again and changed one of the numbers to something I thought it might be. This time the phone went through to an answerphone and it said, 'You are through to the answerphone for the Waltons.' The trouble was, I didn't know her surname; I only knew that she was called Kate, so I didn't know whether it was the right number or not. I put the phone down rather than leave an embarrassing message on what might be the wrong answerphone.

I called back later that afternoon and this time a real person answered ... her dad. He said that Kate was away at horse trials so I realised it must be the right number. I left a message and eventually managed to take her out on a date.

We started seeing one another and got on brilliantly. Kate has a great love of horses and, with my farming background, so do I. I have an interest in a couple of horses now, and through my clothing company we sponsor a horse – Raging Bull Vangelis – but even back then I was a big fan of horses and of horsey people, so Kate and I hit it off straight away. The trouble is, as is always the case with rugby, I wasn't going to be around for very long, because the next tour was just around the corner. This time it was to Argentina and I'd been asked to captain the side. So I said goodbye to my new girlfriend, not sure whether she'd be there when I got back, and prepared to lead England into battle (almost literally, it turns out) in Argentina.

I was obviously hugely honoured to be made captain of the England team, but there was no question that this was going to be a difficult tour. Much like the Tour from Hell in 1998, no one was expecting us to do well as there was, once again, a massively reduced squad with lots of key players not able to make the trip.

People were rushing up to congratulate me on the captaincy, and of course I was chuffed to be asked to be the England captain, but I'm not one of these people who think being captain of England is the be all and end all. I think the real leadership of a team comes from all the guys out there on the pitch and not one person who has been told he is captain. In fact, the truth is that as long as you've got support in the team, leadership is a relatively easy thing to do; there should be leaders all over the pitch. The captaincy is overrated as far as I'm concerned. Much of what is said about the role is tosh. Leadership is about guys taking responsibility on the field.

One thing that you have to do as captain, and one thing that I learnt I had to do very quickly, was to ignore people who were trying to give me advice but didn't know what on earth they were talking about. I knew I couldn't pay attention to people on the outside who didn't really understand what I was doing, and whose opinion I didn't value. You can watch Sky sometimes and hear all sorts of bollocks. Even someone like Stuart Barnes, who's played at international level, will be on television, calling someone stupid for making a mistake. We all make mistakes. He's not stupid. If you listen to those criticisms it does really affect your game. You have to ignore them. The commentator who I do listen to is Michael Lynagh. He will say something like, 'He'll be disappointed with that.' That's right. Lynagh shows a much greater understanding of what it's like at international level. No one makes a mistake on purpose, no one wants to make a mistake, and they're not stupid because they made one bloody mistake. There is this real negativity in England and it's very frustrating.

The other awful thing about being captain is that when things are going badly it is the captain who takes the rap, but when things are going well it's the team that gets the praise. We expect everything from a captain and no one person can do that. It's important to remember that it is a team sport and everyone on the pitch has to take a role when it comes to leadership.

Anyway, enough of my ranting. It just gets on my bloody nerves sometimes. The good thing about the party that was selected to tour Argentina was the great enthusiasm in the side; everyone was thrilled to have been selected and wanted to use the tour to make a mark. There were a lot of guys there who wouldn't normally be on tour, and this was their big moment. There were guys who were thinking to themselves, *We're here, we've got this chance because so many of the others are injured. Let's take every opportunity and use this moment to impress the selectors. Let's not take the easy option*

– *no excuses.* If you are going to captain your country for the first time, they are the sort of people you want to be captaining.

So off we went to Argentina with a group of players that had more enthusiasm than experience, and we arrived in Buenos Aires to discover that Argentina was in the midst of an economic crisis. The banks were in turmoil and none of us could take any money out of the cash-points. There were demonstrations going on all around us because shares had fallen and the government had gone belly up. It was a bloody awful time.

We didn't feel very welcome in Argentina; touring sides from this country never do because there's a lot of hatred towards England sides, all stemming back to the Falkland Islands war of 1982, and the anger that that provoked in people. In 2002 it was the twenty-year anniversary of the conflict, which wasn't a good start, and it was all made much, much worse because England had just knocked Argentina out of the football World Cup.

But we had some fun while we were there, as we always do on rugby tours. I remember being in the room chatting to David Flatman one day when the two of us – the front-row union – decided that we really wanted cream teas and cakes in the room. This was not allowed at all; our food had to be monitored closely, and we were not supposed to order anything in addition to the care-fully nutritionally balanced menu provided by the England team. We weren't having any of that, though, so Flats called down to the reception, put on a funny voice, and pretended to be a coach requesting cream teas. The receptionist refused to allow him any cream teas. She told Flats that the England manager had been very clear that no additional food was to be sent to the players' rooms.

But Flatman insisted that he was a coach requesting cream teas, and not a player, so the woman said she would send up tea and cakes straight away. We were leaping around celebrating our great victory, when the phone rang again. We thought they were checking exactly how much cream we would like, but when Flats answered it, it was Dave Reddin, the England team fitness coach, who had been standing down in reception when our call had come through. He said we couldn't have any more food and that was that – the end of our little feast.

Training was at a minimum on tour; there were so many guys injured that we thought it would be better to keep things very simple in training rather than risk more injuries, so we just ran through basic moves and basic plays and had to hope that when the match came round we would find something within ourselves to rise above all expectations and win. No one was very hopeful, though.

As we travelled to the ground for that first game, we were left in no doubt as to what people thought about us. There were great big signs up everywhere saying how much the Argentinians hated us. When we got to the stadium we found animated fans being held back behind 15m high steel cages.

The game started and they were all over us. We had a penalty inside our own half by the 10m line and Tim Stimpson said, 'I'll kick it.' It sailed between the posts and that was a key point in the game. Everyone was working hard at simple, direct rugby. We decided we were not going to lie down, not get bullied. I felt so proud. Being captain of England in Argentina when they're on a roll is a huge challenge, but when you've got players that will step up to the mark like those guys did it makes you very proud. We won the match and it sent a message back to the guys who weren't there, that they had competition for their places. This was a valuable thing for them to hear, because it ended up lifting the whole squad and making everyone play to the best of their ability. A lot of guys said, 'I'm good. I'm ready for this,' and when we returned to England Clive must have realised that he had far more players to choose from than before we left for Argentina.

The pressure was really on England in the lead up to the World Cup. The media coverage was getting more and more intense. On the whole I think I'm OK with the media. I get on well with the journalists, and I think we have a good, friendly relationship, but there's no doubt that it's hard when you're playing the best you can and giving everything on the pitch, when you read in the paper that England just don't want it enough. That's simply not true. I don't think there's a player in the world who has slipped on that international jersey, sung the national anthem in front of crowds of tens of thousands, then not played as if their life depended on it. The minute I've got that shirt on, I'd die for England.

When it comes to the media, I think I'm very lucky to have been involved with Clive and the England team at a time when all the players had special media training on the things to say and not to say right from the start. Clive was very conscious of how important the media was, and his view was that if you can deal with the journalists and the cameras reasonably well, it takes a lot of the pressure off. Being captain made that even more important for me.

In the autumn of 2002 we had three matches during which we would be able to assess exactly where we stood in the world rankings. The first game was against the All Blacks, now being coached by John Mitchell, who used to coach England. This was a big test for us. Losing to New Zealand in the last World Cup had effectively cost us the tournament. Now, with less than a year to go before the next World Cup, we needed to show that we were better than them. The game began at a frightening pace but Jonny Wilkinson's penalty-kicking kept us in the game so that we went into the break 17–14 up. We survived a late comeback from the Kiwis, ended up with three tries and won 31–28. It was a huge scalp for us.

Australia were next, flying into London full of confidence and with a full-strength side. We won 32–31 in a thrilling contest to lift the 2002 Cook Cup, and make it three victories in a row over Australia. I think this was one of our best games ever, and confidence was really building in the side.

The next weekend it was South Africa ... our third big match in a row, playing all the sides that had previously won World Cups one after the other. We knew we would be playing South Africa in the pool stage of the World Cup so this match was particularly interesting in that respect. We scored seven tries and won 53–3, which was the biggest margin of defeat ever suffered by South Africa in any international match.

On 18 December 2002, for the first time in rugby history, England were ranked No. 1 in the Zurich world rankings.

While all this was going on, I managed to injure my back, and had to have an operation early in 2003, so I missed the 2003 Six Nations tournament. Luckily, I have this great consultant neurosurgeon called Rick Nelson. He's brilliant, and has brought me back from all manner of career-threatening injuries. I completely trust the guy.

It was in February 2003 that Rick was first contacted by Simon Kemp, the England doctor. He wanted to discuss the fact that I had a flare-up of a lower-back problem that had first bothered me back in 1999. I had degenerative disc wear and tear in what the doctors described as the L5-S1 disc. They all agreed it was quite a major problem because I had back pain and sciatica from nerve root compression.

They had given me a scan in 1999 when I'd first suggested that my back was sore, and when Rick looked back at that scan he said there were signs of bulging and narrowing of the disc but not so much that they needed to operate four years previously, just enough to make it clear why I was in so much pain now. By 2003 it had developed into a serious problem and I needed to take action.

So I had my first operation on 28 February 2003. It was what's known as a lumbar micro-discectomy, involving my lower back. It's a pretty standard op, apparently, and was done with keyhole surgery to remove the slipped disc. I had a small incision in my back which was about 2.5cm long to remove the piece of slipped disc that was pushing on the nerve and causing all the pain. The question for the surgeon was what to do with the remaining disc. The discs are there to absorb shock, so they are very important, but a disc will degenerate and lose resilience the more pressure is put on it; it dries out, cracks and wears, and as a result of that pieces of damaged disc push out backwards and onto the nerve root, which is what happened to me.

I know that Rick was very worried about removing too much of the disc because if I had no pressure absorber in my spine and carried on playing rugby I could end up doing myself some serious damage, but in the end he did remove the bits of the disc that appeared to be damaged.

I went back to see him six weeks later, on 11 April, and I had made a fantastic recovery. I think Rick was amazed. 'Do you have no problems at all?' he asked, checking me over.

'Nope,' I replied confidently, bending over and putting both hands on the floor to make my point. Rick looked completely alarmed (and a little bit scared). I was given the all-clear and told I could go back to playing rugby. Rick explained that there was a 5% chance of another disc slipping, and I should bear that in mind. Since 5% didn't seem too bad, I went straight back on the pitch. Rick told me afterwards that he used to wince every time he watched me play and saw me go into contact.

Thanks to Rick and his team, I managed to get myself fit and back in the squad for the build up to the 2003 World Cup and back into the Gloucester side, where things were very different. Philippe Saint-André had left the club and Nigel Melville had come in. I liked Nigel a great deal, and thought it was a huge asset to the club to have someone like him on board, but it was strange to have so many changes going on because every new coach brings in new players.

I remember standing with Wig (Graham Rowntree) after a Gloucester v Leicester match and having a quick pint before we headed home. I told Wig I was disappointed that we'd lost, and he said, 'What do you expect? You've had twenty new players in this year.' Leicester were very consistent at the time, priding themselves on building up the players who were there and not bringing in new coaches and new players every time they were disappointed with things.

With England, in our training for the 2003 World Cup, no stone was left unturned. A vision specialist called Dr Sherylle Calder was brought in to help us with our sports vision as the pressure on us mounted to get fitter and stronger before the trip to Australia. Clive had also brought in ProZone, this very sophisticated match analysis system that would show at every point in the game where every player was. There was no hiding place. Even big fat props would be traced to make sure they covered the necessary ground!

In order to help with my fitness, I was put in the 'fat club', which meant I had to go out on fat-burning runs through Richmond Park. Victor Ubogu was one of the fat club too but he was a walker because he couldn't run. You couldn't get away with anything on these training sessions because Dave Reddin would go with you and make sure you were working hard. It was a killer, and though I hated it like mad at the time there's no doubt that this attitude towards fitness helped set the ground for our success in 2003.

It also might have helped me at Gloucester because we capped a great season there by winning the Powergen Cup, the first Cup win in twenty-five years for the club. We beat Northampton 40–22 in the final at Twickenham. There'd been a confidence in the Gloucester side going into the game, because we'd beaten Northampton the previous two times we'd met them, but they turned up for the match with a hell of a side – fourteen of the team were bloody internationals. But after a close first half, with us 20–22 down, we pulled away in the second half to win by 18 points. The winning of the Cup came after we'd finished 15 points clear at the top of the table at the end of the league season, but lost out to Wasps in the play-off final at Twickenham. It was desperately disappointing not to win that match but there was great satisfaction in coming top and winning the Powergen.

CHAPTER THIRTEEN:

CLUB ENGLAND

In June 2003 the England squad headed to the southern hemisphere for our biggest test before the World Cup. We had a full-strength team and were determined to get the psychological edge before the tournament kicked off. Clive felt very strongly that if we did well on this pre-tournament tour, we'd have a far greater chance of making things work when we arrived in Australia for the World Cup. He was determined that we should go into the World Cup as the team that had beaten everyone else immediately beforehand.

We started off playing the Maori in New Plymouth and beat them easily with our second team. Clive was pleased but not over-enthusiastic. We'd reached the stage with England where we were expecting to win every match we played. We wouldn't indulge in exuberant celebrations until we had the World Cup in our hands.

After the defeat of the Maori, we went on to beat the New Zealand team on their own turf. The last time that had been done was thirty years earlier. The 15–13 scoreline in Wellington represented a historic win for us and we all knew it. Even the New Zealand newspapers were forced to admit that 'the World Cup has just got considerably harder'. Again, we were pleased with the victory, but it felt like a step on the road to a bigger prize.

Next, we moved on to Australia where once again we emerged victorious, this time by 25–14. We outscored the Wallabies by three tries to one as well, which silenced them from saying that we were boring players, at least temporarily. England had never won in Australia and here we were beating them with room to spare just months before the start of the World Cup. It was a great win and set us up brilliantly for the tournament ahead. It gave us a huge lift. Clive had told us that we could do it. These victories would be locked away inside us and used for inspiration once we got to Australia for the World Cup. Every victory now was just adding layers onto our confidence and giving us more and more reason to believe we could win this competition.

It was only five years previously that we'd lost to them 76–0 in Brisbane; now here we were with the positions changed completely and us beating them. After the matches we were all desperate to get home, but Clive was insistent that we make the five-hour flight to Perth to see the hotel that we would be staying in during the early stages of the tournament. He wanted the hotel to feel familiar when we arrived there for the World Cup – just another example of the level of professionalism he was now operating at. Nothing was left to chance, everything had to feel familiar and right. I came back from the tour and went for a two-week holiday in Mauritius where Kate and I relaxed on the beach and enjoyed the time together. I knew that would be the last break I would have until after the World Cup.

I got back from my holiday and we were all straight back into training. The team was getting stronger and stronger from all the fitness work we were doing. It was like training with a club side because we all knew each other so well. You knew other people's scrum machine settings and what they liked and didn't like about training, just like you would in a club environment. I knew the system, the techniques and the personalities. It was Club England, which is exactly what Clive had been keen on achieving. There's no question that he did that. We were all part of a club that felt very familiar and were all very confident.

We went back to work with the Royal Marines before the World Cup again and it was as knackering and as fun as the first time. I remember having to get on this boat called HMS *Havoc* that was filled with foam, water and smoke in order to test me under pressure. They had blocked the holes up so you couldn't see and you had to communicate with each other and work together to get out. The key task was to work as a team. If you didn't, you failed, because you couldn't do it on your own. You learn so much about yourself when you are put in a situation like that.

Clive had started this buddy system with England which meant you were paired up with another player (I was paired with Jason Leonard) and you had to keep an eye out and look out for your buddy to make sure they were OK. I remember this one time in the lead up to the

World Cup, we had an early-morning session that we had to be at. I looked around, but couldn't see Jason anywhere. Everyone else had gathered in the room ready for Clive to start. I knew he had to be there or he would be in trouble, so I went searching everywhere to try and find him.

He wasn't in the reception area, he wasn't in the breakfast room and no one I asked had seen him anywhere. I jumped in the lift and went up to his room where I eventually found him – absolutely steaming drunk, stark bollocks naked, lying on the bed and snoring like a pig.

'Jason, we've got training. Get up. You have to get ready!' Somehow he managed to get himself up out of bed, dressed and in that meeting room in five minutes. He was obviously still drunk but – all credit to him – you'd never have known it. It makes me laugh when I think back to that, because that's clearly not what Clive was intending when he first conceived the buddy system!

I can still picture poor Jason now splashing his face with water to try and wake himself up, before stumbling down the stairs and sitting at the back of the room, quietly. The game's professional, but hopefully some things remain from the amateur days. And to be fair to Jason, he trained along with the rest of us and didn't slack off for a minute even though he must have been feeling like death ... what a true professional.

Training in the build-up to the World Cup involved lots of variations to keep us motivated and switched on. Mountain bike riding was introduced along with my favourite, the war of the rowing machines. There were five in a team for this rowing challenge ... you had to row for 30 minutes as a team and no one was allowed to row for more than a minute so you had to keep swapping. There was a big board put up at the top of the gym wall, and it became very competitive by the end of the week, with players standing and screaming at each other to row faster.

Winning in rugby is all about tiny percentages. That was one of the key messages from Clive. It's not about making huge leaps forward – it would be great if it was, but at elite level no one makes huge leaps forward. It's the tiny little differences that separate the best from the rest. You have to be able to do everything you possibly can as frequently as you possibly can to make those tiny improvements.

One of the things that make good players stand out is their ability to succeed in what we call the fog of war. You have not to get caught up in the bedlam going on all around you. The mental side of the game is crucial. You have to stay focused even when it's going crazy all around you. Discipline is vital. The same way you can't become physically fit overnight, you can't become mentally fit overnight. It takes time. You have to train yourself and put yourself under the greatest pressure, like we did with the Marines.

On a rugby pitch there are about a million different things going through your mind, things that people tell you to remember. It is impossible to remember them all; you need to remember the ones that are absolutely crucial. You have to be aware of other players, the referee, and spaces on the field. When you watch a match afterwards you can see there are spaces everywhere, and you don't understand why they weren't utilised. But sometimes in a match, with all the pressures that brings, you don't see the spaces. That's where the work of the vision experts came in, along with our superior fitness and ability to cope under pressure. It felt as if everything had been thought of, and nothing had been left to chance.

We flew to Australia, landing in Perth on 2 October, and immediately found that Clive had been described as the new Douglas Jardine. He was the least popular man ever to arrive in Australia. That was fine by us and it was fine by Clive. He liked the fact that he bothered them. I liked the fact that they were worried enough to start calling him names and trying to put him off.

Next, all the jokes began about England being too old and too slow. They seemed to have short memories. We'd been here just a few months previously and beaten them. If we were old and slow, what did that make them?

We had ten days to acclimatise before our first match, which was against Georgia. We would also face South Africa in the pool, and like the All Blacks match in 1999 we all knew that game had to be won if England were to have a chance of making it to the final.

Because we arrived in Australia as the No. 1 ranked side in the world, none of us were worried about whether we could win the World Cup, but I remember being concerned that we might have peaked too early. There's no denying the team was getting older, hence all the articles in the papers, and it would have been such a shame if it turned out that we had played all our great rugby a year before the World Cup. It was almost like there was this responsibility not to let that happen, and not to let this golden opportunity pass. It's strange when you're in a set-up like that, full of self-belief, because you always feel like you're letting yourself down if you don't get to the top.

Certainly it seemed that there was no chance of the team being together for the next World Cup, so this one offered our one chance for glory. We had done well as a team but we wanted to win something – that's what the team needed. There was much talk about how we were breaking new ground in taking the sport to a new level; that was all well and good, but what the players wanted was a victory to confirm that this new level was genuine.

Against Georgia, Clive took the unusual decision of playing a full side in the game even though we were due to play South Africa next, and we knew that that would be a very tough game. We won 84–6 against Georgia, running in 12 tries. Georgia were a good side, though, and beating England was obviously something they were eager to do, so they played their hearts out.

Next up was South Africa, and the pressure on us to win was huge. We took the lead early in the match when Jonny kicked a penalty and held on to emerge with a 25–6 victory. It was a huge relief. There was no celebrating or dancing in the streets, just a few job well done's and it was back to business. We hadn't topped the table yet; we still had Samoa and Uruguay to play in the pool. Having said that, the team we had been most worried about had been beaten and a lot of pressure lifted after that game.

We flew to Melbourne for the match against Samoa, and quite a few players were rested for the game, including me. I was on the bench. It looked as if that plan might backfire early in the game when Samoa scored first to go 10-0 up, but England pulled back and we were trailing just 16-13 at the break. I came on for the last quarter of the game and, believe it or not, I scored! We won 35-22, which was a relief more than anything else, and it was nice to have been able to contribute with a try.

There was a bit of a performance after the Samoa game because England had sixteen men on the pitch at one time. Dave Reddin, our fitness expert who had been managing the touchline for England, had let Dan Luger on the pitch when Mike Tindall came off injured, only for Tindall to go back on, meaning that there were sixteen players on the pitch for about thirty seconds. It really wasn't such a big deal because no advantage had been gained from it, but England risked disciplinary action in the week leading up to the match against Uruguay. In the end, England were handed a fine of £10,000 and Otis (our nickname for Dave Reddin) was banned from the touchline for two games.

The final pool game was against Uruguay, and I was captaining the team. There were so many guys in the side with more experience than me, but I was determined to be a good leader. I remember us all standing in a hotel room before the game having a team meeting with the players. Clive came in and the coaches came in and we went through all the detail of what we were to expect from the day and what we might encounter from Uruguay.

Clive did his thing and summed up what the coaches expected of us. He walked out and I felt that, as captain, I ought to say something to the team, so I looked at them and said, 'Now forget about all that bollocks and go out there and play and enjoy it.' I got a round of applause. I think Clive heard the applause outside and thought I'd given a stirring speech! I think the first rule of leadership is to be yourself, and I felt it was important for the players to relax, smile, and remember why we were all doing this in the first place – for the love of the game. We went on to beat Uruguay and qualify for the quarter-final at the top of our group, which earned us a meeting with Wales. So far in the World Cup we hadn't played particularly well, but we were very proving hard to beat. As we would prove to be in the next games, as the tournament started to get more serious.

CHAPTER FOURTEEN:

2003 WORLD CHAMPIONS

Martin Johnson was a great captain during the World Cup, and the main reason he was so successful was because he trusted people to get on with their jobs. The thing with Johno is that he never says a lot. He has a quiet confidence, and you trust him to be there for you if anything goes wrong. You know that he'll give every last drop of blood in his body for the players on the pitch, but he really doesn't say very much.

In 2003 there were so many guys in the England team who were great leaders on the pitch in their own right because of all the experience we had. Johno's great contribution was to believe in them and let them do their job properly. He wasn't some commanding officer charging around giving out advice and instructions to anyone and everyone who got in his way. If he'd been like that, England wouldn't have been anywhere near as successful.

Johno is a very personable guy. Don't let those big lips and big eyebrows put you off ... he might look bloody stupid, but he's very bright. When you listen to what he says, and the advice he gives people if they ask for it, you hear that he makes a lot of sense. The predictions he makes are never far off the mark. He knows a lot about the game. He understands what's happening on the pitch, and he's a good listener; he takes in everything going on around him.

As the tournament moved into the final stages, I felt relief that we were finally here and getting on with the World Cup. It felt like a time bomb in the build up to it, to be honest. I was fed up of talking about it. I just wanted to get on and play. For the later stages of the World Cup I felt like I was in prison – we couldn't leave the team hotel unless we were going to training sessions, and all the conversations were about rugby. People think that rugby's a very sociable game and full of fun nights out and drinking, but I promise you – when you're a professional player in the final stages of a World Cup, you don't do anything except train, go to team meetings and try to kill time by watching TV and chatting to the other players. It's not exactly rock 'n' roll.

The good news was that Kate came out for the last two weeks. It was nice to be able to have conversations with someone that weren't all about rugby and all about the World Cup. I admit that when Kate arrived we sneaked out for dinner on a couple of occasions. Because of the sort of numpty I am, instead of sneaking out to one of the many fabulous seafood restaurants and having champagne, oysters and lobster, I snuck out to a café round the corner where we had sausages, mash and onion gravy and a big mug of tea. I loved those nights. Also my sister, Helen, was backpacking over there with her boyfriend David who she went on to marry, so it was great to see them too and to hear about their trip.

For the quarter-final against Wales in Brisbane, the pressure was really building, and the players were getting tired. All the training and the early games do start to add up; I remember feeling so tired that I spent the whole time wanting to sleep. If you keep training and playing and don't get enough sleep, it catches up with you by half-time and you start to feel exhausted.

In this quarter-final match we were told to keep everything calm, and not to get frustrated. Clive kept saying, 'Remember what we talked about. We've just got to win this game.' There's no doubt that we all backed ourselves to win because of what we'd been through earlier, but the trouble with World Cups is that by the time you get to the quarter-final stage, it's knock-out rugby. It's all about what happens on the day. It's a one-off game ... a cup final in its own right. There are no second chances. Your tournament is over if you don't win it. We were all aware that we would have eighty minutes of sheer hell to play through and we had to emerge victorious.

We fielded a full-strength side for the match and were quietly confident. Wales played a great game, though, and, to be honest, in the first half we were falling apart. It's hard to pinpoint exactly what was wrong. Whether we were all just exhausted, weighed down by expectation, or worrying about the next match ... there's no question that we played worse in that game than we had for ages. By half-time we were 10–3 down. As we went back into the changing room for the break, we were all aware that if we didn't pick things up in the second half we would all be on a plane back to England in the morning.

We pulled ourselves together and the next forty minutes was a different affair altogether. We showed much more confidence and stopped making all the silly mistakes that had been tripping us up in the first half, and we won 28–17. It was a healthy reminder to us all that the World Cup was far from won and if we lost concentration for a minute we'd be out of the tournament and on the way home.

We performed well under great pressure in the second half, but there were still two games to go and we would have to play like our lives depended on it if we were going to win the World Cup. We knew that all the training and everything we'd been through would only be worth it if we actually won something. That's what we would be remembered for. No one says, 'He was a good player.' They'll say, 'He was a good player – he won the World Cup.' We needed the trophy in our hands if we were to consider ourselves a truly great side.

The next day we boarded the plane to go to Sydney for the semi-final. Now we were at the serious end of the tournament, with France looking to settle old scores by beating us and creating a World Cup shock, as they had in 1999 when they beat New Zealand. France are a team that can create a bit of magic on their day so you're never quite sure what to expect from them. We had to make sure it wasn't their day.

On the coach on the way to the ground, there was lightning and pouring rain. I know what the French are like when the weather is bad, so as the rain started sheeting down against the window of the coach I admit that I allowed myself a little smile and thought, *They could struggle in this,* which cheered me up. There are lots of French players at Gloucester (thanks to the earlier influence of Philippe Saint-André) and I know what they're like when the weather isn't good. I've seen them really struggle in the rain; they much prefer the sunshine and hard grounds. It was only a little thing, but the sight of that rain pouring down made me feel a little bit more confident and certainly more determined that we could get the better of them.

We needed to feel confident because there's no doubt that the semi-final was a big match for us because France were being billed as the form team of the tournament. They had won all their games prior to the semi-final very comfortably, unlike us. There were murmurs that England weren't playing their best rugby, with people suggesting that we were too old and had peaked during our tour to New Zealand and Australia the previous summer. We interpreted the whole situation very differently. We felt that France hadn't yet been tested in the tournament, and that's why they had won all their games easily. It's never a good thing to go through a tournament without being tested in the opening stages and we all knew that. We felt we could beat them.

When we ran out for the game, the one thing I'll never forget is seeing the wall of white shirts. It was incredible and so motivating. The stadium holds 80,000 people and the vast majority must have been English. It buoyed me up massively to see all those people there – dressed in white and waving white flags.

We didn't have the best start to the game, going behind early on when a lineout throw didn't hit the target and was deflected out of our line for Serge Betsen to take and score. At first we weren't sure whether he'd grounded the ball or dropped it, but the video referee confirmed that it was a try and Freddie Michalak converted. The great thing about the team then was that we didn't panic. We stayed strong and stayed confident and came back through two penalties from Jonny Wilkinson. You could feel the French players sink back as Jonny slotted the kicks over. It was pouring with rain and France couldn't play the lively, open game they wanted to, and appeared to have no other options.

The game was played in the sort of weather that was crying out for short targets, and with Jonny in the team we knew we could do that. We managed to win the match without scoring a try, which is something we wouldn't normally boast about, but in a World Cup semi-final, in weather like that, it was the right way to play. Jonny was incredible. His kicks just wound the French up more and more as they struggled to make any inroads themselves and became frustrated. With the growing frustration came the penalties, which an on-form Jonny was able to convert. We were 12–7 up at half-time and won the match 24–7 after a ruthless second half in which we continued to kick to put them under pressure.

It was definitely our best game of the World Cup so far, even though we didn't score a try, because we didn't give

Gentle touch from the prop-forward: These two baby porkers are in a safe pair of hands as Phil Vickery gets down to some farming chores. *Picture: CHRIS HOLD*

Village's oval ball ovation

GRAHAM ANDREWS reports

A VILLAGE with a population of under 1,000 has cheered on no fewer than five young rugby stars to national or county glory in the season that's just ended.

The loudest applause to echo around Kilkhampton went to teenager Phil Vickery who rose to the dizzy heights of an England Under-16 prop-forward.

His front-row colleague Peter Risdon, 17, turned out for Cornwall Colts and the three scrum-half Nancekivell brothers, Richard, 24, Roland, 22, and Edward, 16, also found fame in county colours — and, in Richard's case, a third visit to Twickenham in four years.

Phil, all 16 stone and 6ft of him, is rated so highly by the England selectors that they kept a place open for him after a groin strain during training ruined his chances of playing against Italy and in Spain.

Proud

He and his England teammates eventually lost 22-0 to Wales u/16s, though this has in no way diminished the delight from Budehaven School, where Phil is swatting for his GCSEs.

"He is the first rugby player at our school to play for England and we're very proud of him," says PE teacher Nick Wilson. "The selectors rated him as their No 1 prop and he shows great potential.

"Now he must decide whether to make something more of his rugby career, bearing in mind his farming and travel commitments."

Phil, 16, lives at Killock Farm, Kilkhampton, and is the son of Barry and Elaine Vickery. At 13 he was the baby of the Bude Colts team.

His skills on the field were quickly spotted by the county, to Devon-and-Cornwall combined, to South West, to South and ultimately into the full national squad, skippering the side in one of the earlier matches.

As he goes about keeping himself fit down on the farm, Phil says of his hopes for an England Colts cap: "You always have to hope and go out with the right attitude. But there's a lot more competition for Colts places, so I'll give it all I've got and hope I'm no noticed."

As to the Nancekivells, from Heatham Farm, Richard — he plays for Northampton — was back at "Twickers" yet again, but failed in his bid to repeat last year's epic County Championship when he scored twice against Yorkshire. This time he collected a beaten finalists' medal — at the expense of Lancashire.

Promise

Brother Roland, meanwhile, progressed from Cornwall u/21s line-up in 90-91 to the county B team, while Phil's colleague Edward, 16, showed much promise in Cornwall u/16s, as did Peter Risdon, of Collaton Farm, in the No 3 jersey.

The only sad part in all the celebrations is that the man who coached all five stars — and indeed put the Nancekivells' father Dave through his paces too — did not live to see their achievement.

Former long-serving Bude teacher Ivan Opie, 62, died in November after battling against cancer, having come out of retirement to train Phil and Edward.

● Kilk has also shone under the female sporting spotlight thanks to Sally Jeffery, who fought her way into Cornwall's u/21 netball team — at just 14.

ove: I should have been a model! My brother rk and I smile sweetly for the camera.

jht: Making a right pig's ear of things. Local wspapers loved to bring the fact that I was armer into their reports.

low: I was never a fan of diets! This is me, right, at a golf tournament.

Above: It's my ball and you're not having it. A raging bull for Gloucester.

Below: The England pack triumphant over Scotland at Twickenham in the 2001 Six Nations.

Above: Three Lions, 2001. I was always so proud to pull on the red shirt.

Right: Coach and captain: Brian Ashton is one of the best coaches I have ever worked with. He understands the game inside out and back-to-front.

Left: Me with Clive Woodward – the man who masterminded the World Cup victory in 2003. I learnt a great deal about the importance of detail from him.

Above: Our victory down under against Australia in June 2003 made us believe we could really win the World Cup.

Right: Me in full flight, ball in hand, bursting through the defence. Take note, Jonny Wilkinson!

Below: A proud moment: me with my great friend and team-mate, Lawrence Dallaglio, as we are driven through London with the World Cup. Special times.

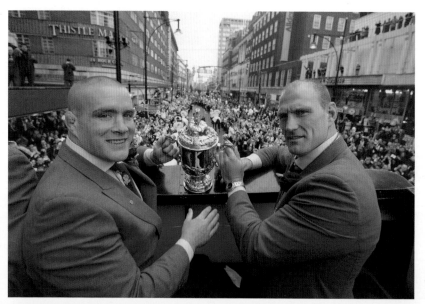

ove: Bodies everywhere, but
 got the ball. My try against
uth Africa, at Twickenham,
?006.

ow: Try! The tubby farmer from
rnwall scores his first for England,
ainst Samoa in the 2003 World Cup.

Above: My beautiful daughter,
Megan, in one hand, and the
Heineken Cup in the other,
after beating Leicester in
the 2007 final. Life doesn't
get much better than this.

Left: An interesting tackle. No wonder I've had so many neck injuries.

Right: A proud man. I love my country and was delighted to have an opportunity to wave the flag as England beat France in the 2007 World Cup semi-finals.

Left: The dark art: the moment before the two front rows meet is a tense time, but I love it. Here I am playing for Wasps in 2008.

Above: Holding the massive Guinness Premiership trophy in 2008 with Lawrence. Winning it with Wasps was really special.

Right: I may have been captain of the Lions against Western Province in 2009, but I still wanted to take my cuddly toy with me.

Left: In your face: I've got the ball, and I'm not letting some South African get in my way.

Above: Time to relax. This is what life's all about – on holiday with Kate and Megan.

Below: My world: Megan and Harry, my beautiful children.

the French any space or time to play their game, and mentally we felt as if we had the better of them because of the conditions. It was a great win for England, and suddenly here we were, with just one match between us and the World Cup.

The lead up to the World Cup final against Australia was unbelievable – I've never known anything like it in my life. The hotel was surrounded by fans, singing and chanting throughout the day, and every time we tried to leave to go training fans would come running towards the coach from all directions, waving, singing and wishing us good luck. I'd never seen so many white shirts before. Everyone seemed to be dressed in the England shirt.

Lots of people were ringing up the hotel to wish us good luck in the competition, and there were lots of good luck messages in the room from the Queen and various international coaches and players. That week training was scaled right down because the last thing we wanted was for anyone to get injured before the match, and we were all exhausted, clinging on in there, holding back injuries, just trying to get through the match. We were about to break. It's a bloody good job the match came when it did, and we were peaking at the right time. If there had been any more matches before the final, I can't say for sure how many of us would have survived.

Despite the excitement, the tremendous amount of support, and all the letters and faxes flooding in to the hotel from celebrities, politicians and members of the Royal family, the week really dragged leading up to the match because we couldn't leave the hotel. It became deadly boring to sit around, counting the minutes down every day, just wishing match day would arrive. I found I couldn't sleep, which didn't help. I do have trouble sleeping at the best of times, because I'm one of life's worriers, and under the pressure of the big match and everything it meant to so many people, getting to sleep was almost impossible.

When match day finally arrived, I think everyone in the camp was relieved that it was finally here. No one had any terrible illnesses or injuries, and we were ready to get out there and get the match played. In the week leading up to the game I'd thought a lot about what to expect from the scrum and how I was going to play it, but in the end you know you've just got to get out there, cross your bloody fingers, plough in there and get on with it, so you don't want to think too much or you'll send yourself loopy. One thing that's hard when you think about the scrum is that you can swing madly between feeling thrilled and excited and convinced that you're going to be all over them in the match, to feeling, *Oh God, this is a nightmare. Did you see how he tore so and so apart in the match last week ... shit this is awful.*

All emotions are heightened and, honestly, you can send yourself round the bend. The other thing you have to remember is that rugby's a team game and the scrum is about all the forwards, not just the props – you have to work together and share the responsibility and the accolades. It's no good me going in there like a bull in a china shop and charging with all my might when the others aren't ready or engaged. We have to work together.

Finally it was time for us to go. Clive said his bit in the hotel and Johno stood up to say a few words. They were filming everything at the time, and Johno made them take the cameras out of the room because he wanted to talk to us and say some very personal things that he didn't necessarily want captured on camera. 'This is why we're here. We have earned the right to play in this match. We have earned the right to win the World Cup final.' There was nothing that needed to be said, to be honest. It was all quite calm and laid-back, which was as it should be. If you need pumping up for the World Cup final then something's gone seriously wrong somewhere. It was emotional but there was no shouting at all, it was more about calming yourself down than hyping yourself up.

We ran out onto the pitch and all I could see was white and gold everywhere. It was amazing to be so far from home and have such great support. I'm sure that around 40% of the crowd was English, which is astonishing considering how far from home we were. I couldn't quite believe that we were finally there – in the World Cup final – after everything that had happened. All the defeats, the criticisms, the injuries, the doubting, the travelling, the training and that God-awful fitness work ... all for this moment.

I remember thinking about all the friends who'd be watching the match, and all the people I'd met along the way who had helped me so much in getting me to this position. I thought about how proud they would be of what I've achieved, and that made me feel good. I hoped they'd realise how much they were part of it, from my school teachers and my rugby coaches to my family and friends. I stood there on the pitch, looking out at all these white shirts, and my overwhelming feeling was that I didn't want to let myself down. I am quite an emotional person at the best of times and I was feeling very emotional that day, very passionate about the sport, playing for England, and all these amazing players standing all around me on the pitch. We were in the World Cup final. Bloody hell!

As the national anthems were playing I thought again about all the people who had helped me get here, from the next-door neighbours and Mum and Dad who drove me to matches all around the country, to the people who knew my Nan and Granddad who I'd met over the years. Were they watching now? What did they think of all this? Were they as stunned as I was?

The match started, and it was fast and furious from the beginning. It was raining that evening but that didn't stop the Wallabies from throwing the ball wide right from the beginning and coming at us. They scored early in the game when they kicked to the corner and Lote Tuqiri touched down. It wasn't the start we'd been dreaming of. The only consolation was that they missed the conversion. The other consolation was that, much like in the game against France, we got back on the attack straight away. The real highlight of the first half was when Lawrence Dallaglio made a bursting run around a ruck to pass to Jonny and then to Jason Robinson who ran and dived over the line, skidding into the deadball area with two Wallabies chasing him. The England fans burst into song and all was well with the world. We went in at half-time 14–5 up.

In the second half we knew that Australia would be coming for us and it was important that we kept our shape defensively and made sure there were no gaps for them to skip through. I think we did this well, and Lawrence and I were constantly chatting to one another to make sure there was no space between us big enough for an Australian player to burst through. In fact the only problem we were having was in the scrum where we seemed to be giving away penalties every time we scrummed down.

There was me on one side of the scrum and Trevor Woodman on the other side, and the plan was to go out there and destroy the Australian scrum, which is what we did, but we kept getting penalised. It was a nightmare, and I was aware that all the penalties we were giving away were allowing Australia back into the game. I still don't know what the referee Andre Watson had a problem with, but he said that I was boring in towards the hooker. Since I'd spent sixty minutes of the game looking at their tighthead's head somewhere under Steve Thompson's legs and nothing had been done about it, it seemed a bit rich that he was having problems with my scrummaging technique. I don't care if referees make wrong decisions, as long as they make wrong decisions for both sides.

We were in total and utter confusion because we couldn't work out what we were supposed to do to put things right. Australia had relatively weak props on the field because they'd lost Ben Darwin, their big scrummaging prop, in the semi-final. In the final they played Ali Baxter, who had just a handful of Tests, and Bill Young who's not the strongest of scrummagers. Trevor and I were all over them. It still mystifies me that we went through the whole tournament, scrummaging really well, giving away just one scrum penalty, then all of a sudden we were penalised like that in the final when we'd have no reason to scrummage illegally. He blew for a penalty three times – me for boring a couple of times, and Trevor for not binding. It was bloody frustrating.

The match flew by very quickly. It was scrappy and full of handling errors, and we seemed to be dropping the ball or knocking it on every time we got it. There's no doubt that we were the stronger side in the second half but the silly mistakes allowed them to claw their way back. Jonny tried a couple of drop goals but they went wide and we failed to score in the second half, as Australia got closer. In the dying seconds of the game the score was 14–11. We were still ahead but the gap had closed significantly and the pressure was on. The Aussies had the put-in to a scrum, but as we pushed into them their tighthead collapsed it. In my opinion there's no doubt that the referee should have awarded a penalty to England, and if he had it would have marked the end of the game, but life is never that simple, is it?

The scrum was re-set and a penalty was awarded against us. Elton Flatley kicked the ball through the posts to level the scores as the final whistle went. The match would go into extra time. Clive came over to me and told me that he was taking me off and putting Jason Leonard on to try and sort out the scrum situation. Obviously this was disappointing, but I understood why he had to do it, because we simply couldn't afford to give away any more scrum penalties. Jason managed to calm everything down and not concede any more penalties. He said later,

'I went on and I didn't scrummage.' He said the only way to guarantee not getting any scrum penalties awarded against him was just to lean and hold the scrum and not to push at all. It worked, and with the scrum steady, the game settled. Each side exchanged penalties, with Jonny scoring first to give us a momentary lift, before Australia equalised in the second half. It was 17–17 and we were approaching the end of extra time. If neither side could pull ahead, the World Cup would be decided by sudden death. I sat on the bench, my heart in my throat, willing the guys on with every ounce of my being.

England had just one minute on the clock. Could they possibly do it? I knew they could. The players all knew they could. But I was in the frustrating position of not being able to help them. I sat and watched and then I saw it happen ... the move that would win the Cup. It began with a lineout ... Lewis Moody wins the ball at the back, a ruck forms and you could see the Australians watching Jonny like hawks. They think he is going to go for the drop goal. Matt Dawson realises that all eyes are on Jonny so makes a sharp burst through to give us another 15 metres. But Dawson is trapped at the bottom of a ruck so Neil Back throws himself into the scrum-half position and pops the ball up for Johno, giving Dawson time to get up. There are about thirty seconds on the clock when Dawson approaches over the ball and looks up for Jonny.

With his wrong foot, Jonny kicks the ball towards the posts and it sails through the air in painfully slow motion. Was it ever going to go between the posts? It seemed to take forever. Finally it did. England had taken the lead in the World Cup final with just seconds on the clock. The crowd roared, we all jumped up onto our feet and paced around, but it wasn't over. There was still time on the clock. Around twenty seconds still to go. Australia race back to try and restart the game before England are properly into position but they kick short and my old mate Trevor Woodman catches the restart and sets up a ruck. The ball comes back to Dawson, who holds it for a few vital seconds before getting it out to Mike Catt. Catty belts it into touch, sending it over the head of Will Greenwood, who is, by this stage, crouching down on all fours to keep out of the way of the flying ball. It goes into touch. The whistle goes. The World Cup is ours!

The minutes after the victory were a blur of excitement and sheer joy. The coaches ran onto the pitch with me – the defence coach, attack coach, kicking coach, scrum-maging coach, all these men who had been brought in by Clive. Once they started working with the team, it seemed so obvious that they should be there, but before they arrived no one had considered how much they would improve our game. You have to take your hat off to Clive Woodward. He changed the way the game was played, he raised the bar. Not just for England but for rugby players around the world. Now his hard work had paid off handsomely.

I looked out into the crowd and spotted Kate. She was cheering and shouting along with everyone else. Then I looked across at the players standing next to me. One of the lovely things about team sports is that you become close to people as you go through these incredible experiences with them. The guys who were on the pitch with me that day in 2003 will always be great friends. We have a special bond built up through adversity and the pressure of losing games, as well as touring together, training together and achieving the ultimate victory together.

It was special to win the World Cup. Really special. The thing with an achievement like that is that no one can ever take it off you. That's what made it so special. What-ever happens in life, whatever life throws at me, this chubby farmer's son from Cornwall played a sport that took him around the world and he was paid a good wage for doing it. Now he'd won the World Cup. I started think-ing, as I always do when I'm feeling emotional, of all the people who had got me here in the first place. I thought of the people in Mum's village in Cornwall who look for articles about me in the paper, and push them through her front door, and I thought of my brother who was back in Cornwall and had started playing rugby at the same time as me. Was he proud of what I had achieved? I hoped Mum had enjoyed the match and was proud of me.

After the match, I shook hands with the Australian players. I remembered the way they had behaved when they beat us in 2001 – going mental, leaping into the air and screaming and shouting and going crazy, making gun signals all the time and doing everything in their power to make us aware that they were the winners and we were the losers. After we beat them in the 2003 World Cup final, I did think to myself, *Every dog has its day*. I know that's a terrible cliché but it's true. You've got to enjoy the win, but you can still be respectful, shake your opponent's hand and be civil and gracious in victory. I know that sounds bloody dull, but I do believe you've got to behave properly when you win and when you lose.

CHAPTER FIFTEEN:

AN AUDIENCE WITH THE QUEEN

After the World Cup victory it was a magical, slightly surreal time. We kept muttering, 'We've done it, we've done it, to one another. It was as if we had to keep saying the words in order to believe they were true. I felt like I wanted to share the happiness of victory with everyone around me. Winning the World Cup made us feel relieved as much as anything else. We'd waited so long for this moment, and planned for it in such detail, and so much had been expected of us that it was a huge bloody relief to win the thing.

Because it had been a late kick-off, it was after 1 a.m. by the time we got away from the ground after the post-match press conference. There was a drinks party being held for the teams down in Sydney Harbour, but Kate and I just went back to the hotel. Kate was leaving the next day and I was completely exhausted, so we thought it would be a good opportunity to spend some time together before she left. Even if she hadn't been there, there was no way I could have gone to the party. I was knackered. After the match I felt so physically and mentally exhausted that it was like someone had pulled the plug on me. I was barely able to get myself back to the hotel. I had loads of lovely phone calls and messages from people, congratulating me. It was a very special time, but also a real blur of utter exhaustion and relief.

The next day we had the big International Rugby Board dinner in the evening which was a fairly formal affair full of lots of miserable-looking Australians, who were clearly disappointed not to have won the World Cup, and didn't mind who knew. There were sour faces everywhere.

Finally it was time to head back to London, so we boarded a plane that had been renamed *Sweet Chariot* for our return. Everyone was looking forward to getting back. Despite the fact that we were all so tired, it was still a great flight. We had the Cup with us and went up and down the plane with it, showing it to everyone.

'The plane touched down at 4 a.m., meaning we were woken, half blinking in the harsh light of the aeroplane, at about 2.30 a.m. As we left the plane, we didn't expect anyone to be at the airport to meet us at that time of the morning. To be honest, it hadn't even occurred to me. When we got off and were met by camera crews, I was surprised. I thought they were nuts to have got up and come out so early.

We had to have some photographs taken with sponsors before we were free to go into the terminal building and through to the immigration hall. We were all feeling pretty tired by this time. I was exhausted and hoping to get through quickly so I could go home and see Kate, but as I walked towards the hall I was told I couldn't go through. The players were stopped by the police and told we would have to go down a separate channel. I don't think any of us really thought this was a big deal, and assumed it was usual protocol when a big team lands at an airport.

The police took us down a separate route and suggested we should go into the arrivals hall in groups, rather than all together, but still I didn't think this was odd. I just assumed it was because there were a lot of us with loads of luggage, so it would be better not to descend on the bags all at the same time. Some of the guys were starting to get a bit fed up because they were tired and keen to get to the hotel. Eventually we just thought, *F—k this, we're going through*, so led by Neil Back we marched through, all together.

We entered the arrivals hall not expecting to find anything out of the ordinary and BLOODY HELL ... there were people everywhere. This was silly o'clock in the morning and there were kids there, old people, young people, men and women. Oh, my God! It was unbelievable. I'll never forget the sight of literally thousands and thousands of people cheering us and singing as we walked through. It was incredible. *It was 4 a.m.* England rugby fans are the best supporters in the world, and to see them there, at that ridiculous time in the morning, all out to congratulate us, thank us and celebrate with us was great.

The arrivals hall was a sea of faces, all smiling, as we made our way out to the car park. It took us an hour to get to the coach and even when we drove out of Heathrow we saw people lining the streets, hanging out of car windows, waving flags and shouting their support. One of the policemen told me that an estimated 10,000 people had descended on the airport that morning. The car parks were all so full that many people had just dumped their cars on the sides of the roads, or even on roundabouts. On the road back to Pennyhill Park people were beeping their car horns. It was the most extraordinary welcome home, and that's when I realised, perhaps for the first time, just how much this meant to everyone in England.

Back at the hotel, the staff came out to greet us and cheer us back. I must say a word about the staff of the Pennyhill Park Hotel, because they've been brilliant to us for years and they've been with us all the way. They are part of our team. Though they were congratulating us that morning, we were also keen to thank them for their support. We had breakfast at the hotel, then another press conference before we were free to go. I headed back to Gloucester and when I got there almost collapsed due to complete exhaustion.

Back in Gloucester there was huge World Cup fever. People would cross the road to shake my hand and tell me how much they enjoyed the victory, and tell me where they were when Jonny landed his kick. A cab stopped right next to me one day and a guy jumped out and ran over to shake my hand to thank me for winning the World Cup. He told me that the World Cup final in November 2003 was the best day of his life. Everyone was coming up to me and telling me what they were doing that day, and how they watched the game. It was great to have been part of it, but in some ways, when I heard all their stories, I think it must also have been nice to have been able to sit back and watch it all happen.

I've been told so many tales by people of what they got up to that day. There was one guy who told me about how he went to watch the final and there was a power cut, so they had to phone a friend who put his phone next to the television; then the guy who called had to put his phone next to a loudspeaker so everyone could hear it. People had great tales about what they did that day to make sure they could enjoy the rugby. In reality, though, I wouldn't have wanted to be anywhere else but on the pitch.

I received a rather strange honour when I got back from Australia – I was granted the Freedom of the City of Gloucester which, apparently, due to some old legislation, means I can drive my cattle through the town centre. I haven't tried to do it yet, but I might one day. There have been a lot of jokes about the fact that a dairy farmer is allowed to drive his cattle through the city centre, but in truth I was very flattered. I was sent a scroll with the city's Coat of Arms on it, announcing the honour.

Gloucester Rugby Club had been incredibly supportive of my international career, so when I got back from Australia I headed straight for the club and threw myself immediately back into club rugby. I played against Northampton that Saturday even though I was completely exhausted and drained from the training, playing and travelling. The club hadn't put any pressure on me to come back so quickly, but I really wanted to because everyone had been so supportive of me when I needed the time off for England training. The Gloucester fans mean a lot to me and I knew they would like to see me out in the Gloucester colours soon after returning from the World Cup, so that's what I did. If I'm honest, though, it probably wasn't the best idea to hurl myself back into training so soon after returning. With hindsight I should have taken some time out to get myself fully fit and rested before hurling myself back into club rugby.

In the event, Andy Deacon knocked into me at training on the Tuesday night and gave me quite a bash. I remember being face down in the mud, unable to move, feeling drained and in pain, and thinking that just a few days previously I had been playing in the World Cup final. It was a silly thing to have done, and I suppose I was bound to get injured. I ended up with a rib injury and a smashed eye socket that required surgery – which prevented me from captaining England against the New Zealand Barbarians in December.

A couple of weeks after we got back from Sydney, the England squad were invited to be the guests on a parade through central London. We got together at the Inter-Continental Hotel on Park Lane in December, and it was the first time we'd been together as a team since we flew back from Sydney. There were two double-decker buses that had been redesigned with big pictures of the team on. The plan was for us to get on them as they weaved their way through London, ending up at Trafalgar Square. It was a drizzly, miserable day so we weren't expecting many people to turn up. In the event they estimated that around 1 million people turned out that day to celebrate with us. There were people everywhere and St George's flags flying from buildings, cars and lampposts. The parade was awe-inspiring and crazy. I could never have dreamt that so many people would turn up. I was so pleased to see every one of them.

There was even a ticker-tape parade in Trafalgar Square and it was announced that we would all be made honorary Freemen of the City of London. Sadly, that doesn't allow me to drive cattle through the middle of London!

Next stop was Buckingham Palace. I can't tell you how excited I was to be going to Buckingham Palace to meet the Queen. I'm the most patriotic bloke in the world – there's nothing I like more than standing out on the field with my chest puffed out, singing the national anthem and knowing that I am representing my country. To hear that the Queen of my country had invited us to the Palace was beyond my wildest dreams.

People who are not Royalists might not understand just how much the whole thing meant to me, but I would say that going there to meet her was one of the highlights of my life. She was charming, lovely, and it was such an honour to meet her. It makes me feel emotional just writing about it now. I love my country so much and I am very proud of the Queen and all that she does.

When we first arrived at the Palace, there were people who knew all about protocol who came to tell us how we should greet her when she arrived. They said we should call her 'ma'am' (pronounced like *jam*). We were all practising what we had to say when a door opened and about twenty corgis came running in. Then the Queen appeared. It was all very relaxed and enjoyable, with cucumber sandwiches and tea. She made an effort to come and speak to everyone, which was nice. I have even more respect for her now than I had before, and I'd never have thought that was possible.

It was nice to go to the Palace on an informal occasion like that because it's a very different experience from going to the Palace for a formal function. I went back there to collect my MBE, and whilst I really appreciated the chance to go back, it was much nicer to be there with just a few of us.

We stayed at Buckingham Palace for a good couple of hours and for every minute it was a real privilege to be there. I would say that going to Buckingham Palace meant more to me than anything else. It may sound daft, but I'd have given up everything else just to do that.

After the Palace we all went to an evening champagne reception at 10 Downing Street to meet Tony Blair and Gordon Brown. That was an incredible experience. They were both so friendly and welcoming. Gordon Brown was Chancellor of the Exchequer at the time so we were hassling him to try and get our match fees and win bonuses tax-free, but he wasn't having any of it!

It was great to be going up the stairs and seeing the previous Prime Ministers' pictures on the wall. I took a picture of Winston Churchill on my iPhone that is still there now. I look at it from time to time to remind myself of what I did that day. It's such a privilege to play international rugby and to help fulfil the dreams of millions that when you get to meet these hugely important people on top of it all, you feel very blessed.

I walked into one room and saw the Cabinet table. I had to stop for a minute and think about all the important decisions that had been made around it. I kept thinking of all the people who had sat around that table over the years. Then there was this room at the back which was apparently Winston Churchill's favourite room. What an incredible experience.

After that memorable day there were tons of invitations to dinners and events. It got to the stage where you just couldn't go to everything and had to pick and choose which events to attend. At the end of the year, I achieved the ultimate accolade when I was told that I was to be awarded an MBE.

I have to admit I found it odd to be getting an MBE when there were people at the Palace waiting to be honoured for a lifetime's service to a really good cause ... like caring for others. I kept thinking, *I'm just a rugby player*, and these other people had done so much and deserved to be recognised. I felt humbled and as if I shouldn't have been there. It just reminded me that there are many out there who do very good things with their lives but are hardly recognised most of the time, and how great it is that we have an honours system that pays tribute to their work.

When the Queen arrived she made us all feel so relaxed. Some of the players were taking pictures of her on their mobile phones, which made me laugh. The lovely thing about going to collect my MBE was that I could share it with the family, and it was nice that Mum came with me, along with Kate.

The World Cup was an amazing experience for me. When I see guys from that England World Cup winning today, it makes the hairs stand up on the back of my neck. There's something about them that's very, very special. Whatever else happens to me in my life, I will always treasure the fact that I was part of the team that won the World Cup and I was surrounded by great men. The odd thing is that I have never watched the final. It's one match that we never analysed. We didn't need to take any lessons from it going forward. Winning the World Cup was the dream. We'd done it.

CHAPTER SIXTEEN:

LIFE AFTER CLIVE

Once we had won the World Cup, the pressure on us to be successful mounted. I suppose you could say that we were there to be shot at in some ways. The players were exhausted, many of them carrying injuries, several of them debating retirement, and all of us feeling that we'd peaked for this big game and were still coming down from the high. So, given all that, I guess the first Six Nations after the World Cup was always going to be a tough one. In the end it was tougher than any of us could have realised.

Martin Johnson retired from the game after the World Cup, which hit us hard. When someone like Johno goes, what do you do? How do you find another Martin Johnson? You don't ... it takes time and experience for players to be of that standard. He wasn't someone we could easily replace. Jonny Wilkinson was out through injury for the entire Championships, which was another blow, and for the eleven of us on the pitch who had been in the side that started the World Cup final it meant coming down to earth with a bang.

The 2004 Six Nations wasn't much fun for any of us because I suppose we all thought that training would be freshened up after the victory, and that things would change as we went forward, but when we all got together again we found that it was the same talks being given by the coaches, the same coaching and the same drills. Nothing had changed and there was a feeling of *déjà vu*.

We certainly felt there was extra pressure on us, now that we were World Champions. Everyone always wants to beat England at the best of times, but now everyone also wanted to beat the World Champions, which meant that beating England became more important than ever. It was as if we were expected to perform better than we ever had, despite key players missing and the rest of us having been on a downward spiral since the World Cup.

Time had given the victory some perspective, and we realised how much it had meant to us all. We were keen to do the best we could to hang onto our world title. Sadly, we didn't hang onto our invincible tag for very long. In our first Six Nations game after the World Cup, we lost to Ireland at Twickenham.

My most enduring memory of that match was of Brian O'Driscoll standing up to give his speech at the post-match dinner, and saying, 'If you're World Champions, then what does that make us?' How ungracious, and what a silly thing to say. If you want to be champions of the world then you need to win the World Cup, you can't wait until after the tournament then beat the team that won it. *It doesn't work like that, Brian.* His words hurt at the time, because as a sportsman you want to keep winning for as long as possible after the big victory.

We lost to France in the last game of the championships as well, meaning that we had lost two Six Nations
games. We hadn't done that in all my time as an England
player.

Once the season was over, I had to have an operation
because my back started playing up again. I became
aware of a loss of mobility, particularly in my legs, and I
was really struggling to do even the most basic of exercises at training, and I knew that, pretty soon I'd have to
head back down to Bristol Hospital to meet up with my
old mate Mr Nelson. I first made the journey back to see
Rick, the trusty neurosurgeon who had done so much to
help repair me before the World Cup, in April 2004. He
welcomed me with open arms, of course, and when he
saw the state I was in he did an immediate scan and
decided an operation was needed. I know that Rick
resists performing operations unless they're absolutely
necessary, so when he said he thought it was the best
course of action and that things wouldn't get better by
themselves, I resigned myself to another few months
away from the sport. In the end, it would mean me missing the summer tour to New Zealand and Australia and
not returning to rugby until late in October.

I had the operation on 7 May 2004 and when Rick
operated, he found little fragments of disc material which
he removed. There were also fragments of the edge of
the lining of the disc which had come away and needed
to be removed. The lining is cartilage that protects the
disc from the bones and I knew Rick was worried about
that because the cartilage was there for shock absorp-
tion and if too much of it came away I'd find myself in

trouble. 'We'll need to keep an eye on that,' was his warn-ing. Under repeated impact, the cartilage had loosened. 'We can't allow you to lose too much,' he added.

After the operation, once again I did very well, and recovered much more quickly than anyone had antici-pated. Two months later I went back for a check-up and the only thing I was suffering from was stiffness which, considering everything that my back had been through, wasn't bad. I know that Rick was very relieved to see that I'd come through it all so well.

But while I'd been away from rugby recovering from the injury, everything had changed. Clive had left his role as England manager and Andy Robinson, who had been Clive's deputy throughout the World Cup campaign, became the new England coach.

Andy Robinson becoming the England coach was undoubtedly a good thing. I've worked with Robbo a great deal and I have a huge amount of respect for him. He has a great passion for the game and a will to win. I was pleased when I heard that he was going to be the new England coach because it gave us a great individual at the top of English rugby and it gave us continuity. Andy had been the No. 2 when Clive was running the show, and he knew what we'd all been through, what we were all like as individuals and how we worked together as a group. People think that the players have some say in who becomes coach but that's not true; I just heard on the news like the rest of the public did. There was no phone call or anything. He just started work and that was that.

There's no doubt that when Clive left it became a very different England set-up. Robbo made his mark straight away on the team. There were lots of little things that changed instantly – for instance, we didn't go to Pennyhill Park any more and trained at Bath University instead. That was fine and I understood why Robbo needed to break links with the past, but we did start to feel as if lots of shortcuts were being made everywhere.

Under Clive we'd been used to having our own rooms, but suddenly room sharing was introduced. The standard of food dropped – it wasn't that we were being asked to eat rubbish, it was just that everything under Clive had been done to the nth degree. The accommodation and food had to be perfect ... everything had to be right. I got the impression that many of the changes made by Andy were not because he wanted to do things differently but because he was being made to save money. Travel plans were not as luxurious as they once had been, either, and it felt to me that investment in the team was not like it had been before. It became quite noticeable that corners were being cut and money was being saved, just at the time when we needed to fight with all our might to retain the mantle of world champions.

Louise Ramsay, the team manager, had been a phenomenal organiser and a real positive force in the team. She left, so the organisation and investment in our comfort was being done differently as well. Change is not always a bad thing – far from it. I think the one thing we all thought was vitally important after winning the World Cup was to implement changes to take things on a stage. I know that Andy had been keen to put his own stamp on the England team so of course he had to change things, but we did have this niggling doubt that most of the changes were because investment was withdrawn from him and he was forced into making many of the cutbacks rather than wanting to make them.

Under Clive Woodward there had been a great mix of coaches including Andy Robinson, of course, but also Brian Ashton, who is a very positive coach. Brian encouraged us to play with ambition and freedom within the system. He is one of the best coaches in the world. It always felt like it was a nice balance between the coaches. Brian was often off with the faeries but that was fine, because there was Andy Robinson there to bring him back down to earth again. The players were an experienced bunch by this time as well, so they would put their own spin on it. You ended up having a lot of very experienced players and very experienced coaches working out how the team should be playing. It was a great blend of styles and experiences.

You had Phil Larder, who had a great on-the-field perspective defensively. He was also good at communicating what he wanted and you knew exactly what you had to do. Dave Alred was a fine kicking coach, and Dave Reddin was a brilliant conditioning coach. It was a great environment to be in. You felt as if you could win all the time. It didn't feel as if things had changed dramatically now, it was just that one person had been taken away along with a lot of resources, meaning that we had to do what we did before but without as much input. I felt Andy Robinson was never really given a fair chance in this new austere environment.

As I struggled to get fit again, playing for Gloucester and hoping to get called back to international duty, there was something else in my life that was proving a rather big distraction. Towards the end of 2004 Kate told me that she was pregnant. I was over the moon. I don't think anything in the world has ever excited me more than the prospect of becoming a father.

I was just obsessed with Kate's pregnancy – honestly, it was ridiculous. I went to all the NCT classes and got hold of every book I could find so I could learn all about the pregnancy and what was happening. I couldn't get enough of it. I loved all that detailed stuff about the growing baby, things like 'At week 13 the baby is the size of a grape and it has eyebrows' ... 'Week 16 and the baby's got all its fingers and fingernails.' I just loved it.

I spent a lot of time with Kate that summer, and when Megan was born in July 2005 I remember everything about it. I was there the whole time, I wouldn't have missed it for the world. Kate was fantastic. Megan came out clean, pink and perfect. I cut the cord, which was great. We'd been expecting it to be a boy, so the first thing Kate said was, 'Where's his willy?' and the doctor had to explain that girls don't have willies. I did the old skin-on-skin thing, taking off my shirt so I could lay the baby on my chest. It was wonderful. But scary. This tiny little creature who seemed so vulnerable, and this great big ugly Muppet here was holding her. What if I dropped her?

I remember sitting in the delivery room at the Gloucestershire Royal at one point with this tiny baby in my hands and she started screaming. I had no idea what to do. Kate was in the shower and I didn't want to be a pain and go to the shower and ask her to come out, so I tried to work out what was wrong. In the end, it turned out the baby was hungry, and there was nothing I could do about that since Kate was breastfeeding at the time, so I had to wait until Kate came back to give Megan some milk and then everything was OK. I'll never forget that feeling of vulnerability ... sitting there with a baby crying and not having a clue what to do about it.

I remember leaving the hospital and ringing round a load of people that I hadn't spoken to in years, and telling them the good news that I had a baby girl. The whole thing was wonderful. The birth had seemed so simple and easy. Little did we know that in a few years' time when Megan's brother was born it would be a very different experience.

CHAPTER SEVENTEEN:

A BIZARRE INJURY

I'd love to have been in contention for the Lions tour to New Zealand in 2005. With Clive Woodward as head coach, I knew it would be well organised and run like clockwork and I'd have loved to have had one final tour with Clive before he moved away from rugby and into football, but it was the oddest injury that stopped me in my tracks – not a smash in the scrum to send me scuttling back to Rick Nelson's surgery, but a moment of madness when I whacked my arm down onto Lee Mears's head and broke it. It meant that I couldn't be considered for the tour and faced time at home rehabilitating instead. It also meant lots of time to spend thinking about life, and how unfair it is.

It's strange being an injured rugby player because you're no use to anyone. It's not like having a broken arm if you work in an office – you might not be able to do as much as other people, but you can still get in to work and help out and be part of things. It's different in rugby. You can't train properly, and you can't play in any matches;

not only that, you have to do tons of rehab and reconditioning when you are better, to make sure the arm is back up to full strength.

It's a very difficult time. I guess people might think you have an easy time of it, lounging around in front of the telly, but it's not like that at all. It's incredibly frustrating and very worrying because you don't know whether you ever will come back. What if that's it, and your rugby career's over? What if you never play again?

Thoughts like that keep me awake at night. I don't sleep very well at the best of times and it's worse when I'm injured. It's a bloody pain, to be honest, but I'm the sort of guy who worries at night when everyone else is asleep. As I mentioned before, I'm a terrible worrier. I think about everything at night – rugby, and life, how I'm going to pay the mortgage, whether the kids are OK, everything. I've always been like that, but it definitely got worse when I had Megan and had her and Kate to worry about as well ... suddenly there were three people to be worrying about at night.

I can find myself panicking about the most ridiculous things. Megan was only a few months old and I was worrying about how she was going to buy a house in twenty years' time. It was crazy, and in the cold light of day I'd wonder what the hell was wrong with me, but I'd still lie there at night with things churning through my mind, keeping me awake.

People are always saying that there are two sides to me, and that I'm a very different person on the pitch to off it. I'm a big softy off the pitch. I never fight with people and I like an easy life. Kate and I never raise our voices to one another. We're just not like that. My treasured memories are not of boshing people in rugby matches but of having tea with the Queen and being there for the birth of my daughter. Talk about a right bloody softy ...

The guys at the club have always taken the mickey out of me for the fact that I'm such a soft touch when I'm not on the rugby field. They also think my taste in music is hysterical. I don't know why, because I have very varied tastes. James Taylor is what I like to play in the gym. I drive the boys mad when I put him on. I like classical music, hip hop, jazz and country as well. I enjoy eighties stuff, which winds the guys up. But the thing I get the most stick for is my love of Take That. I think the band's great. One time Kate and I were on the game show *Mr & Mrs* and I said that I'd love to see Take That in concert. But when I went to training afterwards I got so much abuse. They had Take That playing in the gym when I arrived, and were all singing along to it when I walked in. But I won't take it back. I bloody love Take That and I don't care who knows about it.

The thing I like best in life is being outdoors. I'm definitely an outdoor guy at heart. I suppose that's only natural considering I was brought up on a farm and spent so much of my time when I was younger outside. I love the time of year when spring is in the air, the sun comes up earlier and you start to see a real difference in the way the birds behave, like the rooks starting to fight and rebuild their nests. You notice the lambs are in the field and molehills start appearing all around the place. I remember Granddad hated the way the moles would appear and ruin the ground with their little holes.

Whenever I see moles I think of him and how cross it used to make him. I remember that he used to take the soil from the molehills and put it in the flower beds.

I still lead a semi-rural lifestyle, with a big garden and a room-size vegetable plot. I'd like to be more self-suffi-cient one day, and grow lots of vegetables and have lots of animals roaming around. I'd also love to have my own cider press because I've got a forest of old apple trees and it would be great to make my own cider from them. One thing I'm very passionate about and would love to do one day is to reintroduce old trees that are dying out. Trees and plants go in and out of fashion, but there are some beautiful old trees that people don't plant any more. I'd like to start up a big campaign to bring back the lost trees.

I tend to keep my life away from rugby very separate from the sport. There are lots of people within the sport who are good friends and I keep in touch with, like Trevor Woodman, Martin Johnson, Mike Tindall and James Simpson-Daniel. I'll meet up with them maybe three times a year, but I've still got all my other friends who have nothing to do with rugby and I think that's impor-tant. You have to have a life away from rugby. Back in 2005 and 2006, when I was struggling to overcome injury and get myself back into the England team, it was nice to have friends away from the sport who took me at face value for what I was, and not how I was doing in rugby.

Not playing for England because of injury meant I had a lot more time on my hands. Much of it was taken up with the new arrival in the house, as I played a hands-on role looking after Megan, but I also caught up with friends and watched some of the television programmes that I love, like *Holby City* and a bit of *EastEnders*. My favourite shows, though, are programmes like the BBC's *Springwatch*, or anything to do with nature or history. David Attenborough is my hero. I also like cop shows, things like *Cops with Cameras* and *Police Camera Action*. I get a thrill from watching the fast chases and arrests. I guess I'm still a little boy at heart.

One thing I don't do when I'm injured is watch a lot of rugby. I'm not a good watcher of the sport when I should be playing, so I tend to stay away from it. It feels a little bit like rubbing salt into the wounds.

People assume I'm aggressive because I've got a bulldog tattoo on my arm from when I was 19, and a tattoo with Chinese writing that says, 'I will fight you to the death,' that I had done when I was 21. I had the bulldog one done because I wanted to make a statement about being British. It's a British bulldog, and I'm proud of where I come from. The Chinese tattoo is not strictly about fighting someone to the death, it's about the fact that I won't give up. Whatever I'm doing, I won't give up. I may not be the brightest or the cleverest but you can rely on me to give it everything I've got. I love the fact that in two symbols I've managed to say that I'm a grafter who you can rely on and will be there until the bitter end. I suppose another way of looking at it is to say I'm a bit of an idiot and quite stubborn, but that wouldn't have made such a good tattoo!

Away from the rugby field, I'd say that I wasn't madly competitive. I'm not one of these dads who can't even play games with their kids without winning. I love sports but I'm not obsessed with them. I wouldn't even say that I was obsessed with rugby. I think I've got the sport in perspective. I love it and I love the people who play it. I love the lifestyle it has given me, the places it has taken me to and the experiences it has offered me, but if it disappeared tomorrow I'd cope.

Back in 2005 there were many times when I thought rugby was disappearing for me. Lots of people were questioning whether I would ever get back into the England team, and at Gloucester, where they had always been so supportive of me, I could tell they were starting to lose faith. I felt as if the pressure was on me to get fully fit and back at the top of my game, or Gloucester would tire of me and I would end up having to leave the club.

CHAPTER EIGHTEEN:

'WILL I PLAY FOR ENGLAND AGAIN?'

W hat a bloody marvellous start to the year. Before January was out I found myself back in Rick Nelson's consultancy room, telling him that my back was hurting again. This time it wasn't so much the accumulation of pressure that caused the pain, though undoubtedly repeating ramming my head into a scrum wasn't helping. It was because I had been injured in a game playing for Gloucester against Saracens.

I was in serious trouble, and in so much agony. I just couldn't do a thing. I needed surgery to get me out of all the pain I was in, never mind about playing rugby again. *Pain, pain, pain*. It was the same all the time. I couldn't lie down, I couldn't sit, I couldn't stand. It was sheer bloody torture.

Rick Nelson scanned my back, as he had done so many times before, and suggested that my L5-S1 disc – the one that had caused me problems in the past – had degenerated further. There was another piece of slipped disc which was causing a second major disc protrusion.

He explained that the difficulty is that you can get scarring when you have the first disc operation, and that prevents the nerve root moving freely, and it's where the nerve root and the disc are hampered by the scar tissue that you get the worst pain. So, in I went again on 28 January 2006 for yet another operation. I knew it was a technically difficult operation because of the previous slipped disc and the problems that had caused. Clearly the more operations you have, and the more scar tissue, the more dangerous future operations become.

I was in so much pain waiting for the operation, it was horrible. I can still picture the doctor coming in to see me and saying I should take this or that painkiller. When none of those worked he would give me something stronger and say take two every four hours. That soon became four every two hours. It still didn't help. Only morphine worked, and it was like clockwork. I'd get it every four hours and as soon as we hit the end of the third hour the pain would start again. I'd be climbing the walls that last hour while I waited for the next dose. So the night before that last operation I wasn't thinking, *Will I play for England again?* I'd even got past the stage of thinking, *Will I be able to walk the dog or pick up Megan, my baby girl, once I'm out of here?* It had got so bad that all I could think was, *Shit, I've got to get rid of this pain. I can't take this any more.*

Rick performed the operation for me, but even he admitted that he thought it might be an operation too far, and though he hoped to get me back playing rugby he could not be sure. But he did – he freed up the nerve root and I came through it.

Afterwards I was hugely relieved that the worst pain had gone. Just to be able to stretch out my leg and stand up straight seemed a miracle. There was a lot of recuperating to be done, but Megan was only tiny then, so to be able to spend lots of time with her and Kate while I was doing it was just great.

While I was recovering from the injury, in fact for a while before I got injured, it became evident that my future wouldn't be at Gloucester so I needed to start looking at alternatives. I love Gloucester and I particularly love the fans and the passion in the town for the sport, and I found it a very difficult time when I realised that my future in rugby would have to be somewhere else.

I suppose the main reason for me feeling that my club rugby would have to be played elsewhere was that I sensed that many people at Gloucester were getting fed up with the fact that I had had so many injuries. It's very difficult when you're injured as a player. You're desperate to get back, no one is more desperate than you to get fit and back in the team, but there's nothing you can do if you've just had a major operation on your back. You have to take the time needed to recover, build up your fitness again and then get back in the team.

On the other side, I do totally understand how frustrating it is for a club when they are paying you to play for them but you can't do anything. I know they've all got jobs to do and that rugby is now a business and I know how much pressure there is on rugby club funds. I had been at Gloucester for a long time, and had been injured a lot, so it had cost the club a lot of money. It's basic business economics. The finances of the club don't add up if they are paying you but you're not playing in the team.

Yet, from my point of view, as I lay there, in pain and desperate to be back out on the pitch, it was hard to think about the sport in purely business terms because there is so much passion involved in the sport and so much commitment – much of that commitment being with your own body. It's not your fault if you get injured. If you get injured as many times as I did from giving so much of yourself on the pitch, then to feel unwelcome at the club because of that was a bitter pill to swallow.

I'd like to think that I took the higher ground when I felt the pressure from Gloucester. I didn't want to make a big fuss or sour my relationship with them, because I'd had a great number of years playing for them, but I honestly thought I had more great years ahead, and that's what was so frustrating about it. You'll know by now what a soppy idiot I am, so you can imagine how upset I was about the thought of leaving Gloucester and moving somewhere else. But I had to. The question was – where? A lot of people thought I would go to Bath or Bristol. They are great clubs, but it almost felt unfair to the fans of Gloucester if I moved down the road to their biggest rivals. I decided, instead, to look further afield.

I turned down several lucrative offers from local clubs, then in April Wasps made an approach. The more I thought about playing for Wasps, the more I thought that it just might work. I wanted a new challenge and a different environment and I thought that Wasps would give me the best chance of getting myself back to where I wanted to be.

Because I left Gloucester while injured, I never had a final game after which I could say goodbye and thank you to the fans. I felt bad about that. I'd like to thank them for their support over eleven years at Gloucester. It was the passion and enthusiasm of the fans that turned things round for me when I first arrived in Gloucester all those years ago and had been homesick and desperate to return to the farm. It was a real shame that I couldn't say a personal thank you to them, and of course because I left without being able to play one last game I was portrayed badly in the press. It was all very sad really.

I was happy with my decision to move to Wasps, though. Kate and I decided to relocate to Henley-on-Thames, this gorgeous little place just outside London, so I would be closer to the training ground. The fact that I was moving was announced, and I remember sitting at the press conference, next to poor old Chris Wright, the Wasps owner, who kept on being asked whether it was a big gamble to be taking me on. He was defending it and saying I wasn't a gamble at all, but I was thinking, *F—k, yes. It's a major bloody gamble!* But if you're lucky enough to play at a club where people have your best interests at heart and want you to do well, anything can happen.

The people at Wasps were great. I sat down with them and we had a chat about how I was feeling about my injuries. 'Do you want to get back?' I was asked.

'Bloody hell, yes. Of course I want to get back. I desperately want to get back playing,' I replied.

'Well, we'll help you then,' they said.

I felt as if I was surrounded by people who were genuinely working to get me fit and healthy again as soon as possible. I'll never forget the day I went for a medical at Wasps. I hadn't done anything for ages, I was in pain and I was sure they were going to take one look at the state of me and tell me I wasn't welcome there. But actually, much to my relief, I did a load of exercises which involved bending over, stretching and lifting a few light weights, and the fitness coach said, 'You're not as bad as we thought.' That was the best news ever and gave me a huge amount of confidence.

'We'll start you off on a programme, and we'll look after you and make sure you don't do too much too soon,' they said.

When I left the training room and went back to my car, I bumped into Shaun Edwards in the car park. He came over and shook me by the hand. 'We'll get you back as one of the best in the world again,' he said, and just walked away. Bloody hell. He didn't have to say anything, but he said the one thing that I desperately wanted to hear – he had confidence in me and thought I was capable of coming back and getting right to the top of the game again. He hadn't even said hello; those were his only words. Nothing could have been nicer.

After such a great start, things continued to go well at Wasps. The time they put into me was incredible – on the conditioning side of it I always felt as if they would do anything to make life better for me. They were there to get me fitter, and nothing was too much trouble for them. They are great, positive people at Wasps and they worked hard to get me back on my feet again. I'll always be grateful to them for what they did.

It was all very refreshing to be at Wasps after the situation at Kingsholm where I felt that they genuinely didn't believe I would ever get back to fitness. I'd been injured for so long that I think many of them thought my career was over, and when it came to renegotiating my contract with Gloucester they had wanted to change it so that we could spread the risk more evenly between me and them. Basically, the contract wasn't so good for me. Fundamentally, though, I didn't want to sign a contract that seemed to be based on their fear that I would never get back into the game.

The nice thing about being at Wasps was that it felt like a completely fresh start. I wasn't seen as a risky investment but as someone who would be part of the future of the club. Craig Dowd, the Wasps forwards coach, said in the press how excited he was about working with me and added, 'Phil's run of injury has cost him his title as the best in the world, but at Wasps we are looking forward to getting him back to a position where he can compete to regain that title. At some stage every prop has had a bad back. Phil has come to the right club to be looked after and managed. We have every intention of getting him 100% fit.'

Then, in the summer of 2006, on a gorgeous day, at a lovely little church in Gloucester, I got married to Kate. Life seemed complete.

I spent the late summer after the wedding rehabilitating and hoping to get myself into the team and onto the pitch, to confirm the faith that Wasps had in me.

Eventually I did it, and made my début in the 23–13 win over London Irish on 8 October 2006. It was great to be playing again, but you always worry when you come back from injury that you are not going to be quite back at your best. The thing with coming back from injury is that you can't cheat yourself and only play half-heartedly; you have to be fully committed. If not, you're bound to end up injured again. I was pleased with my comeback, particularly the 30-yard dash to the line that I made.

While I had been fighting my way back to fitness with Wasps, England were struggling. I was recalled to the side as a replacement for the third Autumn international against South Africa, in November, but by then they had lost seven of their last seven Tests, including the previous two Autumn internationals, losing 41–20 to New Zealand and 25–18 to Argentina. Andy Robinson's job was under threat, and we faced two tough Tests against the Springboks.

I came on as a replacement in the game, and was thrilled to be back on the pitch, but not half as bloody thrilled as I was to score. A try! Me! Yep, the wobbly farmer went over the line to score a crucial try in our thrilling 23–21 win. Have you ever heard of anything so ridiculous in all your life? Winning the match was a huge relief to the guys who'd suffered defeat after defeat and were being hammered in the press. For me it was great to get back in the swing of things, and even greater to score a try. Now it was seven defeats in the last eight games, which wasn't exactly a record to be proud of, but was at least better than eight defeats out of eight games.

The final Autumn International was another match against South Africa. This time it wasn't so good. We lost 25–14 and Andy Robinson resigned in December. In his place, Brian Ashton, who I knew very well and was a big fan of, was appointed head coach of the England team.

CHAPTER NINETEEN:

BRIAN ASHTON'S ENGLAND

As World Cup year came round again I couldn't believe how much had happened since we had won on that memorable night in 2003. I'd got married, had a baby daughter, had serious back operations, suffered from a broken arm and fractured cheek, and moved to Wasps when Gloucester gave up on me.

A hell of a lot had happened to England too. We'd lost Clive Woodward and Martin Johnson, the coach and captain who had led us to World Cup victory, along with great players like Neil Back and Jason Leonard. Andy Robinson had taken up the reins, then been forced to drop them again, and now Brian Ashton was in the top seat. It had been a rollercoaster few years for all of us.

Despite the misfortunes of the England team, I was feeling pretty good about life. Just eighteen months previously most people felt I wouldn't be able to play another game of rugby ever again. Frankly, there were plenty of people who wanted me to go away because they thought my time was up. I was seen as being a write-off, someone who wouldn't ever be able to come back from so many career-threatening injuries. But I wasn't prepared to just give up. I still loved the game and I always knew deep down that I'd be back, or I'd never have put myself through all that pain like I did. I'm not a bloody masochist.

While people doubted whether I'd ever come back and whether I was going to retire from the sport, I'd always thought to myself, *Why should I pack it in, just because I won a World Cup and then got injured? Why does that have to be the end?* I knew that I had more to give and I certainly knew that I wanted to play on and resume my career with England.

My trust in myself was rewarded when I received a wonderful phone-call in January 2007. I remember it so clearly. I was in the sitting room, playing with Megan and just chilling out, when the phone rang. It was Brian Ashton calling to ask me how I'd feel about becoming England captain. I told him I'd have to think about it. The truth was that I was desperate to do the job, but I had to see how Kate felt. True to form, she backed me all the way. 'If you want to do it, then you must,' she told me. I called Brian back within half an hour and said that I'd take the job on. It was a tough assignment, I was aware of that, because the England team was at a low ebb and had lost a lot of key players, and I'd been out of action for a long time. But I also relished the challenge. I love play- ing for my country. I love England, I think it's the best country in the world, so the idea of captaining them into the World Cup and trying to build them back up again filled me with desire. Bring it on!

I knew that I was going to enjoy working with Brian Ashton because he's a no-frills sort of guy. He's straight talking and uncomplicated – off the pitch and on it. He encourages free-flowing rugby and individuals to step up and be creative on the pitch. He's a great guy to have in a coaching set-up, and I'd always enjoyed working with him. I was looking forward to seeing what life was going to be like for England, now that he was the main man.

We had our first meeting (I don't think it lasted more than eight minutes – Brian was never very keen on meetings) at the Royal Garden Hotel in Kensington and Brian told us how it would be with him in charge. First of all, he wanted everyone to be punctual. He said that was very important to him. But he said that the most important thing was that there were lots of smiles on people's faces. 'I don't want anyone to be grumpy,' he said. 'It's important that we're all happy. OK?' We all nodded slowly. So far, so good.

'Now then,' he added, holding up the black book. The black book had been an important tool of Clive Woodward's. Woody had created a black folder full of rules and codes of conduct of hundreds of pages that he was eager for us to follow as he formed us into a professional team. The black book that Brian held up was full of empty pages. 'You write in this book if you want to write in it,' he said. 'We don't need all these codes of conduct and do's and don'ts. It's up to you as individuals now. And we won't be having half so many meetings either.'

I think we were all a bit shell-shocked, to be honest. We'd had so many years of meetings and rules and codes of conduct that this all felt a bit odd.

'There's one thing we are going to do, though,' he said. 'We're going to have a new slogan, and that slogan is "Shock the World."'

Bloody hell, I thought. *I like that. No – I bloody love that.*

Our opening game of the 2007 Six Nations was against Scotland, and I was running out onto the pitch as captain and as a prop about to win his 50th Test cap. How did that happen? When you play international rugby, you're always cautious to take it one game at a time and just concentrate on the match in front of you. Now, suddenly, despite a host of horrible, nasty old injuries, I was about to win my 50th cap.

We won the match 42–20, as we won all our home games in the RBS 6 Nations that year, beating Italy 20–7 and beating France 26–18. It was in the away games that we struggled.

Our match against Ireland was to be played at Croke Park for the first time. There was a huge amount of press surrounding this game, and a big build-up to it all through the week. Being captain, I was called in to talk about the occasion, and the historical significance of the match being at the scene of the Bloody Sunday shootings.

I didn't know a great deal about the events of Bloody Sunday until the match at Croke Park came on the horizon, then I learnt what a horrible day it had been, with thirty-one people losing their lives. British security forces had opened fire at a Gaelic Football match in Croke Park in 1920, and fourteen Irish civilians had died. This happened following an IRA operation earlier in the day that had resulted in fourteen deaths. That evening three IRA prisoners in Dublin Castle were beaten and killed by their British captors, making it thirty-one dead. It was one of the most significant events to take place during the Irish War of Independence, so obviously it created strong feelings in people which rose to the surface when England were to play Ireland at Croke Park.

Despite all the fears over what would happen on match day, though, when we ran out onto the pitch the atmosphere was unbelievable. There had been all this talk that the crowds would boo when England ran out, but that didn't happen at all. They cheered us and they really cheered Ireland. It was all very good humoured and respectful and I admired the players and fans for that.

It was a good event to be part of because history was being made, and that's always very special but, sadly for us, we lost the game, going down 43–13. Being captain is not a particularly pleasant job when things are not going very well because you have to account for all the team's failings, and take some responsibility for them. People expect you to have all the answers and – let's be honest – no one has all the bloody answers, least of all me.

You just get on and do your job as best you can as captain, but you're not a different person because you've been made captain. Being captain doesn't change you, though the public image of you does change, and people do expect you to be a certain person when you're captain of the team. It's odd. To be straight about it – I still shit the same as the next guy and the shit still stinks. Just because you're captain, you're not this wizard who knows all things and can do all things. I was happy to be captain under Brian because he's a good guy, but I think way too much is made of the whole captaincy role and what it really means in modern-day rugby.

We lost our other away match – to Wales at the Millennium Stadium. A 27–18 defeat put us third in the table, with the World Cup coming up. It wasn't the most convincing display from the reigning World Champions, and people were keen to point that out. There wasn't much optimism circling around the England team. Brian remained true to his belief that we would cause a shock come the World Cup, and the players remained confident, but the papers were full of gloom and doom.

There were times when I asked myself why I was doing this. When you've achieved victory in the World Cup, why put yourself through trying to come back time and time again? Why? I'll tell you why – because I love it. That's why I do it.

The build-up to the 2007 World Cup was very different to the 2003 tournament. We were staying down at Bath University, and even though the university has great facilities it was very different from the more luxurious surroundings of Pennyhill Park. There was a good atmosphere in camp, and we had a good bunch of boys there which helped us to feel positive about the tournament.

We were told to gather at Bournemouth Airport where we were getting a flight to Portugal. *Great,* I thought. *A few days in the sun. Just what I need.* I headed down to the airport, pulled into the car park and wandered into the departures building, feeling very excited about the fun-filled days ahead. I should have known better.

No sooner were we all assembled than Viv Brown, the team manager, called us to order and told us that the plane was cancelled. She was accompanied by a physical training instructor from the Royal Marines. Oh God. My dreams of a sunshine flight to Faro were suddenly burst in front of me and replaced by the prospect of four gruelling days of commando training. Happily, we did get to go on to Portugal afterwards, although there wasn't too much lying around in the sun – it was all four-times-a-day training sessions in the sticky warmth.

It was a difficult time before the World Cup because the weight of expectation on us was huge because we were defending our world title, while everyone was slagging us off in the papers saying we had shit players and rubbish coaches. Everything about us was criticised. I'm quite good at taking the higher ground, and ignoring it, but it still bothers you when this happens. Everyone wants to do well. No one wants to be on the losing team. You don't want to just go to the World Cup ticking boxes; you want to win the thing.

Brian kept saying, 'If you guys don't believe, it won't happen.' We knew that we had to stay positive in the face of the constant sniping at us, and believe that we were going to win the World Cup.

I was feeling confident after a great season with Wasps that had ended with us winning the Heineken Cup. We had finished top in our group, so we qualified with a home quarter-final against Leinster which we won 35–13 in front of a packed Adams Park. The semi-final was held in Coventry where we beat Northampton 30–13. Suddenly we were in the Heineken Cup final against Leicester.

We knew that the Cup final would be tough because Leicester were in fine form, having already won the

Powergen Cup and crushed Gloucester in the Premiership play-off final. Suddenly they were being spoken
about as the best-ever Leicester side and one that
deserved to win all three trophies. Their coach, Pat
Howard, was returning to Australia at the end of the
season and there was a sense that it was only right that
he should return with all the accolades in the English
domestic game under his belt. As you can imagine, at
Wasps we were getting pretty peed off with this talk, and
the fact that people seemed to think that we were worthy
fall guys for Leicester. This was not the way we saw
things.

One difficulty for us was that we had three weeks without a game before the big showdown, while Leicester
were preparing and playing in the Premiership final. We
tried to organise a practice game against Bath in order to
keep ourselves match-fit, but they weren't keen so we
ended up arranging to play our own second team. This
sounds like an odd thing to do but it actually worked very
well when Tony Spreadbury, a well-known referee, was
brought in to take charge of the game, held at Henley,
and we told him to make sure the second team were
allowed to get away with all sorts of misbehaviour at the
breakdown. We told Spreaders that he could let them lie
over the ball and penalise us constantly, even when we'd
done nothing wrong.

It was a great exercise to do – to have this referee who
was making it extremely hard for us all the time, and
making sure we had to battle constantly. We were
expecting to have to fight in the final itself, so why not
mimic fighting conditions in training? We didn't want to

be bullied into submission by all the talk about how great Leicester were. We were great too, even when all the odds were stacked against us as they were in that training match.

Selection-wise there was one difficulty in the team and that was in the front row, on the other side of the scrum to me. Tim Payne was absent through injury and there was a big debate about who should replace him in the front row alongside me and Rafael Ibanez.

A lot of people thought that I should move to Tim's place at loosehead prop so that I could take on Leicester's Julian White, who is a very powerful scrummager. I was more than happy to do that – I'll play anywhere – but a lot of people, including Lawrence Dallaglio, didn't think that was the right thing to do. They felt it would be wrong to switch me. In the end we turned to our scrummaging coach, Craig Dowd, the former New Zealand great. He stopped all the debate by saying, 'Why would we move one of the best tighthead props to loosehead to try to counter their strong guy?' He wasn't at all interested in us messing around with our front row to try and outplay Leicester. I think that was a good philosophy. You've got to play your strongest cards.

It was decided that by leaving me in my best position – tighthead – there would only be one problem to deal with. There was a feeling that me in my preferred position would give us a chance of gaining an advantage on that side of the scrum, forcing the referee to watch both sides. In the end, Tom French, a relatively unknown player who'd been playing at loosehead for our second XV, was put into the team. The thinking behind this was that, first and foremost, Tom was a good player who we all believed would rise to the occasion, and secondly Tom was relatively small and Craig Dowd had noticed that Julian didn't always seem that comfortable scrumming down against smaller guys. Leicester like to force the opposition upwards and get a lot of penalties based on the perception of their superior scrum but it's much harder to do that against smaller props. We reckoned that any missing bulk in the front row was more than made up for by the heavyweight presence of me and Rafael Ibanez. One thing that really impressed me about Tom French was his temperament through the build-up. You'd think he'd be nervous stepping into the first team for the biggest match of his life, but he was totally calm and seemed utterly unfazed by the task facing him.

Having three weeks to prepare without distraction allowed us to think long and hard about our tactics and what would work best against Leicester. There were all sorts of statistics flying around. In particular, we worked out that in all previous Wasps v Leicester games the team that was leading at half-time invariably won the match. We realised that we would have to get on top of Leicester from the first whistle, to get points on the board, then never let up. It sounds basic when I write it like that, but we knew it wouldn't be easy because Leicester would be trying to do the same. The key for them would be to get in front and force us to chase the game.

The match started and I knew that everyone was worried about how Tom would cope against Julian White. In fact the only person who seemed totally unworried about Tom's abilities in this respect was Tom himself who looked completely unfazed by it all. In the end, it was quite a way into the first half before the first scrum was awarded and by that time we were 3–0 up and Tom was right into the game.

Tom did brilliantly in the scrums, getting right under Julian and preventing him doing any damage to our scrum. This happened in scrum after scrum, giving us such a psychological lift. We led 13–9 at half-time and increased that to 25–9 before the end of the game.

All credit to Leicester, who'd had a fantastic season, but we were the better side on the day. Confronted by our aggressive tackling and our good organisation, they couldn't cope, and we were in control for most of the match. It was an extraordinary occasion, with over 81,000 people crammed into Twickenham for the game, making it a world record crowd for a club match.

I remember standing on the pitch, with Megan in my arms, with all the supporters cheering and clapping. There were fans from lots of different club sides there that day, as well as the core of Wasps supporters, because lots of people buy their tickets a long way in advance in the hope that their team will get to the final, and when their team doesn't make it they go anyway, so it becomes like a great big festival of rugby. It's a great occasion to play in and was a great one to win, after all I'd been through.

After that, it was back to England business, and to the preparations for the World Cup. We had two warm-up games at Twickenham – against Wales and France. We beat Wales 62–5, then lost to France 21–15. Losing at fortress Twickenham is always a difficult thing to take.

We're proud of our home record and hate to lose matches there. We then played France in Marseille and lost 22–9. Brian Ashton kept urging us to be positive and to believe that we could win, but it was bloody hard to do so at times.

CHAPTER TWENTY:

2007 WORLD CUP ... AGAINST ALL ODDS

The first match of the World Cup was against USA in Lens. The build up to the match was vastly different from anything we had for the 2003 World Cup. Brian is a very laissez-faire, relaxed sort of bloke who wants the players to assert themselves as individuals, and not be dictated to, so he didn't come in and tell us what to do before matches, but urged us to suggest what we thought ought to be done. He also asked us to keep things simple, so we didn't give anything away ahead of the South Africa game – our big match of the pool – six days later.

Some of the players found his coaching style quite difficult to get to grips with because he didn't assert himself on us anywhere near as much as Clive and Robbo had done previously. I didn't have any problems, to be fair. I just think Brian was different from other coaches, and took a bit of getting used to. In the minds of many of the players, they associated success and achievement with the Clive Woodward way of doing things, and when coaching and preparation were done in a very different way they immediately became worried. The mood in the camp wasn't helped by the fact that Jonny Wilkinson rolled his ankle in training and damaged his ankle ligaments, meaning he would miss the first game, and possibly others, depending on how his injury healed.

We won the match 28–10 to get our campaign off to a victorious start, but it wasn't a great match. We didn't set the world on fire, and we certainly didn't 'Shock the World' as Brian wanted. Not by a long way. We'd gone into our shells during the match and there was a sense that people didn't really know what was expected of them on the pitch. We'd always been very clear, in the past, about what the management wanted us to do. Not this time … Things weren't helped when, after the match, I was charged with a deliberate trip on Paul Emerick. I hadn't deliberately tripped anyone – I'm just not like that. I play hard and I play to win but I never play dirty. It's not in my make-up and it was bloody awful to have this charge against me. The players all rose up in support of me and spoke out to say I was one of the most honest players they knew. I appreciated that. The truth of the matter is that I was wrong-footed in the game, tried to reposition myself and caught the American centre on his knee. It was a fall, a mistake and not at all malicious. But it resulted in me being suspended for two matches. I was the England captain and would have to sit out the next two matches of the World Cup.

The second game was the big one … we were playing South Africa at Stade de France. I would have to sit the match out because of my suspension, Jonny was still out with his injury and, as if that wasn't enough, Olly Barkley had pulled up in training, meaning that the replacement fly-half was out. Some of the players were getting restless and fed up with the way the squad was being organised. They thought the squad was 'rudderless' without a strong leadership figure. I'd hear them complain that there was no communication and they didn't know what they were supposed to be doing. It was a tough time for me – being a captain who couldn't play, in a squad that was starting to feel unsettled.

The match against South Africa did nothing to settle people's nerves as we went down 36–0, dealing a severe blow to our hopes of successfully defending the World Cup. It was the first World Cup defeat for England since Jannie de Beer had kicked five drop-goals in the 1999 quarter-finals. That had been a desperately miserable time. Now here we were again, losing to South Africa in the World Cup. To be on the sidelines, watching it all happen, made it all the more dismal.

We never looked like winning the match, and trailed South Africa throughout the game, with the Boks scoring tries through Juan Smith and J. P. Pietersen in the first half to leave us 20–0 down at half-time. South Africa continued to dominate after the break as Pietersen went over for a second try, while Percy Montgomery added his boot to the damage by kicking a total of 18 points. The only time we came close to scoring was when Mike Catt missed with a long-range drop-goal.

The annoying thing for us was that even though South Africa had beaten us by a considerable margin, they hadn't played at all flamboyantly. You could even say they had a fairly conservative game plan, choosing to rain a series of high kicks down on Jason Robinson which enabled them to play the game deep in England territory. We let them dictate the pattern of the game – why? What was going wrong? Why didn't we seem to know what we were doing out there?

The guys came off the pitch feeling angry and frustrated. It was the first time since the Tour from Hell that we had not registered a point and every player in the side knew that he could do better. After the match, the anger, resentment and frustration that had been bubbling rose to the surface, and we left the Stade de France in a very sombre mood.

A crisis meeting of the squad was called for the following morning, and we headed for it feeling fairly low but emerged from it feeling lifted and determined. It's funny how much a terrible defeat can end up being the thing that spurs you to great heights, rather than drags you down. The match had been a bloody disaster, but sometimes when you're at an all-time low the only way to go is up. You're faced with two options when you're down on the floor: you either get up, stand up and fight, or you die. The meeting would make the difference between us resigning ourselves to a World Cup death and getting up and fighting for our lives.

It's funny that 'the meeting' became such a turning point during the World Cup, because the truth is that it wasn't a terribly aggressive, confrontational meeting, but a reasonable exchange of views. The meeting would end up getting tons of publicity, but it wasn't that aggressive at all. I've been in far more confrontational meetings in the past.

So, in we all trooped for the meeting and the first thing that happened was Brian asking why the guys had called 'off-the-top-ball' at our second lineout. He said it was the wrong decision. Mike Catt immediately disagreed with Brian. The others agreed. It was as if people wanted to have an argument to get their frustrations off their chests.

Catt turned to Brian and appealed to him to coach the way he usually coached. 'Please coach us the way you know how to,' he said. It wasn't nasty, personal or vindictive, as was reported in the press, but one passionate player, appealing to one passionate coach.

Brian is a great coach, and the meeting galvanised him and made him think. The reason we changed in our attitude after that meeting wasn't because the players threatened or shouted, but because we all started singing off the same hymn sheet. Before the meeting we had felt a little like a pub team on tour. Once we made the decision that we'd had enough of playing average rugby, and we were determined to win, our game lifted and we got stuck in. We believed again ... and so did Brian ... and we all believed the same thing – that if we sorted ourselves out we could win this World Cup.

The next game was against Samoa. We knew that a defeat to the Pacific Islanders would signal the end of our World Cup dreams. We had to win this game, and the great thing was that the change in attitude throughout the squad meant that we believed we could win this game, which we did 44–22.

Our final pool game was against Tonga, which meant we were playing three tough, hard-tackling teams in succession – South Africa, Samoa and Tonga. The pressure on us to win was immense. It was like knock-out rugby – if we'd lost we were on the flight home. We'd beaten Tonga 101–10 last time we'd met them, but knew that in a one-off match anything could happen. Before the game the Tonga player, Epi Taione, claimed that 'all the angels in heaven' were willing his team to win. At one stage in the match it looked as if he might be right, as he flew past Jonny Wilkinson before passing to Sukanaivalu Hufanga to go over. We were trailing 10–3 and it really wasn't the start we'd been hoping for. We won the match 36–20 in the end, which put us through to the quarter-final against our old foes, the team we had narrowly beaten to win the World Cup four years previously ... Australia.

There weren't many people in the world giving us any chance against Australia, but I think within the squad we were more hopeful and more confident than we had been in a long time.

We took the TGV south out of Paris to Marseille where we would be playing the game, all of us feeling fairly positive about life and confident that we could beat Australia. We might have been the only people in the world who believed that, but it didn't matter. We were the underdogs but we were determined underdogs.

The following morning we had a non-contact training session and things fell apart a bit when I clattered into Olly Barkley and gave him a dead leg. Andy Farrell pulled a calf muscle minutes later while chasing a kick. It was all going pear shaped. There were injuries everywhere. The physios were working 24/7 to get players pieced together and back into action. It was like a war room in there. Players were being held together with glue and double-sided sticky tape and were absolutely exhausted.

We were also staying in the dodgiest hotel in Marseille, which served as a marked contrast to the hotels in which we'd stayed in 2003. Still, our spirit remained, and though beating Australia seemed like a long shot we were like a cornered animal – beaten from all sides by bad publicity, criticisms from other players and other teams and rocked by injuries. Cornered animals can be dangerous, though, as Australia were about to find out.

There was massive support from England fans at this stage in the tournament, to encourage and inspire us. I remember having dinner with my wife and with Andy Farrell and his wife the day before the game against Australia. It was early in the evening, around 6.30 p.m. We were tucked out of the way in the corner of the restaurant, and by 9 p.m. we stood up to leave. We didn't think we'd be spotted in there but as we stood up the whole restaurant erupted into shouting, cheering and clapping. They sang 'Swing Low'. It was amazing. If we hadn't been fired up to beat the Australians before that, I certainly was afterwards. Marseille is a great little place in which to play rugby because there's this really pretty little harbour, with restaurants and bars and a great spirit there. Everyone is crammed into this small place so you get a great atmosphere. What happened that evening was awesome.

Even more awesome, though, was the match itself in which our pack ground Australia down and allowed

Jonny to score 12 points to win the game and become the World Cup's all-time leading points-scorer.

It was a bloody fantastic game of rugby and I was so proud of the guys in the team, particularly Andrew Sheridan and Mark Regan who were in the front row with me. We pulverised Australia at the scrum and laid the platform for the back-row trio of Lewis Moody, Martin Corry and Nick Easter to nullify George Smith, the Australian flanker, and deny them ball.

The match didn't start too brilliantly, though, with Stirling Mortlock getting a penalty to give Australia an early lead. Then there was an unlucky bounce from Mike Catt's kick into the right-hand corner which denied Paul Sackey the chance to score our opening try.

But in the rest of the game there was lots to cheer. Some of the highlights for me were the trademark Jason Robinson burst through the defensive line, and Matthew Tait sweeping across the field towards the Australia try line. We were playing extremely well, much better than we had all tournament, but despite all our efforts the only change to the scoreline was two penalties from Jonny.

The Wallabies scored a try through Tuqiri after he slipped through the grasp of Josh Lewsey, and Mortlock converted to put them four points up at the break, but still we felt like we had the measure of the game, and the measure of Australia.

Early in the second half it looked like us lumps in the pack had set up England's first try when Gregan was smothered by Lewis Moody, but with the try-line within reach Jonny's pass caught Catt unawares and he knocked on. Although the attack failed to produce a try, Jonny kicked another penalty to reduce the deficit to 10–9.

Australia were trying to re-establish themselves in the game when Rocky Elsom was panicked into conceding a penalty. Jonny slotted it over to give England the lead. But it was a narrow lead, and there was a panic in the dying moments of the game when Mortlock suddenly had a chance to snatch victory for Australia with a penalty, but it was not to be and we could breathe a sigh of relief. It was our biggest result since the 2003 World Cup final. I felt eight foot tall as we walked off the pitch.

We had beaten Australia 12–10, our determination having been magnified under the enormous pressure of the occasion. The team was full of good guys who were determined to win and prove our detractors wrong. Now we were in the semi-final, while Australia were left licking their wounds. They hadn't booked flights home because they didn't think they'd need them, so confident were they of beating us. When we heard that, it made victory all the sweeter.

The semi-final of the World Cup would be against France, the host team, determined to do what their football team had done previously, and win the Cup on home soil. France came into the match having beaten New Zealand a week earlier, and were playing an England side that they had beaten twice in August, so they were odds-on favourites to send us packing, but still we retained optimism. We were on a roll, we were playing well as the underdogs; in fact I'd say it was much more fun being the underdogs in the tournament than it ever was being the favourites to win and playing under the pressure of expectation in every match.

Before the match I got the guys in a huddle to talk to them. I get quite emotional in team talks. 'You are very, very lucky to do what you do. You will be remembered for doing something. Think about your family and friends. Think of what this means to them. Think of how proud they'll be of you.' I always try to engage with people's emotions in team talks, not necessarily head-butting and screaming. I play my best when I'm wound up emotionally, so that's the way I appeal to the players when I captain.

On this occasion, I think it might have worked. We beat France 14–9 and knocked the host side and one of the favourites to lift the Cup out of the competition. It was another great match for England in which we had an explosive start, taking the lead after just seventy-eight seconds when Josh Lewsey took advantage of a slip by Damien Traille to win the ball and blast over and through the Frenchman to score. It was a stunning start for us but we knew that it would result in the French redoubling their efforts. They did this by playing with width and pace, forcing us to battle against a series of attacks before an infringement at the ruck gave fly-half Beauxis a penalty which he successfully kicked to make it 5–3 after just seven minutes.

We felt as if we were in the driving seat in the game but a penalty for France meant they had edged into the lead. Beauxis missed three long-range drop-goal attempts while Jonny was off target with a similar attempt for us, but France were still ahead as we went into the break.

At half time I told the players not to panic. The game was ours for the taking as long as we stayed calm and did what we did best. After the break, France edged further ahead through Beauxis's third penalty after England again infringed at a ruck, but that was the end of their scoring as we hit back with Jonny's boot as he landed his 50th World Cup penalty to make it 9–8, followed by a further penalty and a drop goal three minutes later. France threw everything they had at us in a series of desperate late attacks, but we held them back to win 14–9. I could barely believe it. We'd defied all the odds.

I have to confess that I felt a bit sad for Raphael Ibanez when the final whistle went. Call me soft, but he was this amazing player who had led his country so brilliantly and had been knocking on a place in the final just as he was retiring from the game. This was to be his moment – retiring on top of the world, leading France to World Cup victory. I desperately wanted us to win that match but I also didn't want Raphael to lose. I know that's dead soppy of me, but I felt sorry for my Wasps team-mate afterwards. I knew a lot had been expected of him because the football team won the World Cup when France hosted it, and the same was expected of the rugby players. Losing was not an option for these guys, yet they'd lost, and Raphael's face was a stark reminder of the difference between winning and losing.

There were a few injury problems for us afterwards, to ladle the pressure onto the physios, with Mike Catt and Josh Lewsey in pieces, but nothing could dampen our spirits. We were in the World Cup final. Few would have imagined us being here when the tournament began, but here we were, preparing to face South Africa, the side to which we had lost so heavily earlier in the tournament, prompting us to re-think everything and confront the problems in the team. It was odd that we were meeting, on a high, a team that had previously sent us crashing so low. For the first time, I sensed genuine optimism outside the squad – from the newspaper journalists who'd previously written us off – that we might just be able to do this, and become the first team in history to win the World Cup for the second tournament in succession.

The feeling in the camp before kick-off was very different to that of four years previously in 2003 when we'd prepared ourselves to face Australia. Back then, there was the weight of expectation on our shoulders; it felt like everyone in England expected us to win, and it was almost as if not winning the World Cup would be a national disaster. In 2007, the mood was different. There was far less pressure, less tension in the air. For me, as captain, this helped a great deal. I had a group of players who desperately wanted to win, for one another, for their families, friends and their country, but they weren't scared rigid by the thought of what would appear in the papers if they didn't. I enjoyed the build-up to the 2007 final much more than I had in 2003.

The match began well for us. We managed to keep the ball in their half for much of the opening period which gave us a real confidence. Where we really struggled, though, and an area which cost us dear, was in the line-outs. We couldn't even win our own ball. South Africa, on the other hand, had really got their act together when it came to the lineout. We had seen enough videos of their previous games, prior to the final, to know that their line-out was very good, so we had worked on ways of coun-teracting this, but in the end our work came to nothing as they made their mark immediately and won our first two lineout throws. This meant we couldn't take full advan-tage of the early possession we had, and Percy Mont-gomery (the tournament's leading points' scorer) kicked them into the lead.

We managed to stay calm, even though we'd been very clear before the match that we wanted to get ourselves onto the scoreboard first, and Jonny equalised with a penalty from right out near the touchline.

South Africa came back at us with another penalty after Lewis Moody tripped Butch James, the Springboks' fly-half, but, besides that, we had a pretty good run for most of the rest of the period, and were heading towards half-time feeling confident. We could win this match, and retain the title. We could do it, there was no doubt about it. That's when South Africa came to life.

Luckily for us, they missed a penalty kick, before John Smit, the South Africa captain, got to within a metre of the line before he was stopped. The last thing we needed was for them to score just before the break because, psycho-logically, that would have been shattering after we'd held them back so well. In the event they managed a penalty before the whistle went, making it 9–3 at half-time.

Although it was a match dominated by kicks, there were a few try-scoring opportunities for us. Just two minutes into the second half, Taity caught a bouncing pass from Andy Gomersall in midfield and raced for the

South African line. It looked like he was going over for the first try of the 2007 World Cup final but he was stopped just short. He passed out to Mark Cueto who dived over in the corner. We thought he'd scored, and had 10 seconds of wild celebrations until the referee turned to the television match official who decreed that Mark had a foot in touch. It was desperately disappointing.

Jonny kicked a penalty goal to pull back three points, but a fourth penalty for Percy Montgomery gave them a six-point lead again. We were lagging behind and it was proving difficult to catch them up, but we kept reminding ourselves that six points was nothing ... two penalties and we would be equal, a converted try and we would be champions again. We certainly weren't out of it, not by a long way.

Brian brought on a host of replacements towards the end of the half, to make sure we had the fittest legs on the pitch for the final onslaught, but then Francois Steyn kicked a penalty for South Africa and took his team ahead of us by more than a converted try. It was 15–6 and the clock was ticking down. Now the pressure was on us.

We put up an almighty fight in the last minutes of the game, but there's no question that our problems in the lineout, and problems in securing the ball at the breakdown, made it very difficult to force ourselves on them.

In the end I think the final was a match too far. It was a narrow victory for South Africa and we could all be proud of the way we played, but still it hurt to come so close and to lose. In so many ways this tournament had been more emotional than the last one. Somehow it meant more because we'd found something inside ourselves that had propelled us to victory, rather than in 2003 when it had been organised so thoroughly for us. The disappointment of seeing John Smit with the trophy was crushing. But despite our sorrow at losing in the final, there was no doubt that the whole journey we went through had been incredible.

Many, many people had criticised and doubted us and we'd proven them all wrong. I felt so proud of the players and the supporters. They gave everything and, as captain, that's all you can ever ask for. We hadn't won the World Cup but we could hold our heads high.

It had been a brilliant trip full of high emotions. The tour had been like the film *Cool Runnings* – this group of guys battling against the odds. It was all about searching inside ourselves to find the strength to win.

The turnaround made by the players was unbelievable. People think that the meeting was the turning point, but the truth is that losing to South Africa was the turning point. We didn't change things in a meeting, but in ourselves. We all started stepping forward and taking responsibility ... the players and the coaches.

A lot was written about Brian Ashton and his alleged shortcomings, but what we did on the pitch was exactly what he had asked us to do. Much of what he wanted wasn't told to us properly, that was the only criticism you could make, but he sorted that out when he realised exactly what was needed.

Brian was always very much of the mindset that you have to play what's in front of you. He believed that players can be over-coached and then don't react in the right way. I can totally see his point of view; we are grown-ups, not children. If there is a five-on-two down the blindside and someone is calling for it, you can't say, 'Sorry, I can't pass to you. We have to go three phases before that.' In Brian's world, if someone calls for it because they believe something's on, you have to trust them and go with it. You have to believe in your team-mates. Rugby's an instinctive game. Of course you have to be coached, but no coach knows what's going to happen on the pitch in the middle of a match. Players have to be able to react to events as they unfold, and that's the point Brian tried to make.

If a player like Paul Sackey gets the ball with three guys in front of him and thinks he can make something out of it, you have to go with him and give him that chance. The game is so structured these days that you need someone who will create a bit of magic and play outside the box. That's what Brian wanted to encourage ... the magicians in the team.

Brian wanted to let us be the players we were supposed to be while giving us every opportunity to be the best we could. Even though we'd had problems on the tour, I was still a big fan of Brian and thought he was one of the best rugby coaches and one of the cleverest men I'd ever worked with.

We flew back to England and went to a press conference at Twickenham before splitting up. I remember Sky's Graham Simmons coming up to me on the pitch and asking me what England needed now. 'We need stability,' I said. 'That's what we need more than anything.'

I drove back to Gloucester that night and next morning woke to debates in the newspapers over how long Ashton would survive, and within six months he'd gone.

CHAPTER TWENTY-ONE:

WINNING WASPS

When I came back from the World Cup I started to get pains in my neck again. A scrum had collapsed when I was playing against Australia and it had been giving me a bit of gyp ever since. I'd coped with painkillers and physio thanks to the England medical team, but now I was back home I knew I'd have to make the familiar trip to Rick Nelson's office to have yet another scan. I'd buggered my lower back so many times in the past that it was probably time for something to go wrong further up. The scan results came back, and guess what? The disc was bulging. I think I have a spine full of bulging discs. This time it was the lower disc in my neck that was causing the problems, and giving me – literally – a pain in the neck.

Luckily, it settled down with treatment from Rick that didn't involve me having an operation, so that was a huge relief, but I was warned that I may have problems with it further down the line – and sure enough I did, two years later. But back in 2007 I was given the (sort of) all-clear and I carried on playing rugby.

The 2008 Six Nations was an odd one. I always find them strange after World Cup years because so many key players retire after big championships, so suddenly you're without key anchors in the team. After 2003 we had lost Johno and Neil Back, among others; now we'd lost Lawrence Dallaglio and Mike Catt. I played every game in the championships except for in the 23–19 win over Italy which I missed through injury.

First up were Wales. Much like in the Six Nations after the 2003 World Cup, we lost in our first game, going down 26–19 to them at Twickenham. Much was made of this at the time. If you peak for a World Cup final, then of course it's going to be downhill after that, especially when you consider how many top-class players we lost to retirement afterwards. It's daft for any team to start judging itself immediately when a World Cup competition is over.

We were all over Wales in the first forty minutes, and were playing some good rugby, then Wales turned it around in the second half and came back at us. It was such a 'game of two halves' that it was untrue. At half-time Warren Gatland, the Wales coach, said, 'What do we say to the players? They can't get near the ball.' He was right. Wales couldn't get near us, we were dominating in that first half, and it was frustrating that we allowed them back into the game and couldn't finish them off.

I think we'd all got the feeling that Brian Ashton was vulnerable during the World Cup, and certainly afterwards, every time there was a defeat, like with the Wales game, there'd be someone somewhere calling for his head. I felt quite sad about it all. Brian and Andy

Robinson are two of the best coaches I've ever worked with, yet it was like there was this gun pointing at Brian all the way through the championships.

The next match was against Italy in Rome where we came away with a 23–19 victory. I hate playing against Italy because they're always better than people give them credit for, and you have to be very careful or they'll get the better of you. It was particularly hard for the guys playing them in 2008 because everyone was so negative about the way we were playing, and we worried that one defeat would mark the end of Brian's career, or prompt a complete overhaul of the team. We just wanted to settle down and get some matches under our belts with the new guys in the team. We didn't want any rushed changes or forced resignations.

We didn't play massive rugby in the Six Nations, but no one else did either. It's not that we didn't want to play a great, expansive game. We have this dream about running rugby and wanting to play the best rugby we can, but sometimes you just need to play winning rugby.

Next up was France, in Paris. This was our first meeting with them since the Rugby World Cup. So it was a big revenge match but we just took it for what it was and didn't allow ourselves to get too het up, and we won 24–13. Next up was Scotland in a match that was affected by the fact that Danny Cipriani was missing because he had been photographed coming out of a club the night before. I think that whole incident was extremely tricky for Brian, who'd told us all to get an early night. He reacted swiftly and strongly, and told Danny he wasn't in the team. It was very frustrating and I felt cross with

Cipriani. We were beaten on the day fair and square, going down 15–9.

In the next game, against Ireland at Twickenham, Danny was back in the side with a lot to prove. He had a storming game and we battered Ireland. We did everything that Brian asked of us and finished the tournament on a high, with a 33–10 win, giving us second place in the table. It wasn't enough to save Brian. A few weeks later Martin Johnson was announced as the new manager of the England team and Brian was sacked from his job as England head coach.

I hated the way in which Brian was treated. All the debates began over who would be the new England coach while he was still in place. It was as if he wasn't there at all. It was very disrespectful towards one of the best coaches in the world.

If the RFU wanted him to go, they could have spoken to him, and allowed him to go with more dignity before they started looking for a replacement. It was about decency, and the way the thing was handled was a bad reflection on everyone involved. They say it's a professional sport but some old-fashioned manners don't go amiss. Brian did some heroic things for England, and that ought not to be forgotten. When Brian was eventually sacked, the way it was done was all wrong. I've stayed in touch with Brian, and I hope we'll always be friends. He's a decent man, and the sort of person you want to count as a friend.

What I liked about Brian was that he was selfless. The game wasn't about him, it was about the players and making sure they felt good, and had the confidence to do the things they had to do to win. Some of his ideas were up in the clouds – he would reach for the ultimate in the hope that we'd get close to perfection, and that's a great mentality for a coach to have. He always used to joke with me that when his friends in his local asked him what his proudest moment was, he'd say it was when I got the ball in a match one time and tapped and passed. He loved that. He loved that under his control of the team every player felt they had the confidence to play the ball as they found it. Even the props.

As Brian went out, so Johno was settling himself in. A lot of people have asked whether it's strange going from playing with a player to being coached by him, but to be honest it's not, because it happens all the time. Most coaches are former players. We get used to it. One of the first things Martin did when he became England coach was to give me a call to say, 'You are not going to be captain.' Johno is a friend so I guess it is quite hard to take a call like that from a friend.

He had rung me up before he was appointed coach when he had been talking to Rob Andrew and discussing the new role. He asked me whether I thought he should take it and I said, 'Are you asking me as a fellow player or a friend? Because, if you're asking me as a fellow player, I would say take it. As a friend, I'd say don't touch it with a barge pole.'

Johno was the World Cup winning captain. He was bulletproof and the man everyone wanted in their team. Why take it when the chances were he was taking on a poisoned chalice? The next week Johno signed for England and dropped me as captain, so I'm not sure how much notice he took of my advice. Yes I do – no f—king notice at all.

It doesn't wreck friendships when things like that happen, though. You have to separate friendships from business, and I still thought of Johno as a friend. I respected his need to make the decision that he thought was right for the team ... even if I thought that decision was wrong.

When Johno became manager, not much changed immediately because we still had the same coaches beneath him in the England set-up. Brian Smith came in as attack coach; he was the biggest change. Everything else stayed pretty much the same.

Coming in to coach the England team with no experi-ence of coaching was a huge risk for Johno and would heap massive pressure on his shoulders, but I never worried about that too much, because Martin Johnson and pressure go together like peas and carrots. I've seen the man under huge pressure and he doesn't bow.

I was disappointed to lose the captaincy because it's a real honour to do it, but it can't be forever, and if you get yourself het up about captaincy you need to stop and take a good look at yourself. I think people who go searching for the captaincy are very vain and something is wrong with them. You should be aiming to be the best player you can be, and if you're made captain – so be it – enjoy it. But if you crave something you have no control of and can't ever guarantee getting, you're never going to be very happy. Control what you can control; concen-trate on being the best player you can be, not on whether someone makes an arbitrary decision to make you captain. Anyway, being captain is great when you're winning, but it's a lonely old place when you lose 43–13 to Ireland at Croke Park. Trust me – I know.

The one thing that I did really like about captaincy was that I learnt a lot about myself. I learnt that I love the game and was much tougher, mentally, than I'd realised. I began to look at things differently and realise that it's not just about you in your position on the field, but about everyone, the whole team coming together and making the thing work. But, also, I learnt that unless every individual does his own little job to the best of his ability then there is no great, big team effort. It's very much about a game of individuals pulling together, selflessly, for the good of the team.

The other thing that my time as captain confirmed for me was that the game is very emotional. I have to get into an emotional state to play well. As captain I think I said it how it was, and was always true to myself. I also learnt that if you start reciting lines from movies you need to give yourself a shake because people will fall away. You have to speak from your heart and soul. Then you've got them. Then you're captaining.

At Wasps we were having a storming season. We had been lying about tenth in the league a couple of months after the season kicked off, with most of our leading players caught up in the World Cup and unavailable for club action, but once the cavalry returned from the tournament in France the fighting spirit kicked in and we stormed up the table. We lost only two more games in the entire season to top the Premiership, and had to face our old nemesis Leicester in the Guinness Premiership final. Leicester had won the title the previous year and we knew how eager they would be to retain it. They would also be gunning for us after we beat them to win the Heineken Cup the previous year. There was everything to play for in this game.

The match started with Mark van Gisbergen and Andy Goode exchanging early penalties before we had our first meaningful attack, and I was involved. I turned myself into ball-carrier for a brief moment as the Leicester defence seemed to fall apart. We took advantage of their confusion for Tom Rees to dive over for a try that Mark VG converted from the touchline.

We could sense straight away that Leicester felt under pressure from this early try and moved into a defensive pattern of play. They had one roar back, briefly, through Alesana Tuilagi, but we hadn't quite finished with them, and ended the opening half with a 10-point blitz in six minutes thanks to Josh Lewsey's try. This came about through a missed tackle by Tigers flanker Ben Herring that allowed Josh to sprint clear and touch down, with Mark's fifth successful kick giving us a 23–6 lead at the break.

Van Gisbergen was a star for us, managing to add 16 points to our total. His opposite number for Leicester, Andy Goode, managed to score just 2 from six attempts which made a huge difference to the scores. Without a kicker on form, the game becomes very hard for every-one else on the pitch, and the opposition realise they can exploit this weakness. We certainly did that. You sense real vulnerability in a side when the kicker's not convert-ing the penalties you're awarded.

Because of my lack of match fitness, I stood aside and made way for Pat Barnard to take my place on the pitch at the break, so I watched the rest of the match from the stands. Leicester were desperately trying to come back at us in the second half and they threw everything our way from the restart. Territorially, they stayed with us, but if I'm honest, their lack of firepower was exposed until Goode finally got through after fifty-six minutes with a clever cross-kick that caused uncertainty in our defence. Tom Varndell pounced for an opportunist score.

Varndell's touchdown only reduced the gap to 23–11 because Goode missed the conversion, but Leicester were back in the game, setting up a nerve-tingling closing fifteen minutes. A kick from the great van Gisbergen put us 26–16 clear, and when Goode missed a straightforward penalty nine minutes from time the game was over. We had won.

I was particularly pleased that we managed to mark the end of the 2007–8 season with a victory because this season signalled the end of Lawrence Dallaglio's career. As well as being a great rugby player and inspirational team-mate, Lawrence is also a great guy and I'm proud to have played alongside him. I mentioned earlier that he strode out to meet me when I first turned up to play for England, and shook my hand and welcomed me in a gesture I still remember today. He's a decent and honourable guy and someone I hope I'll stay friends with long after we've both given up playing rugby. Wasps' victory meant they had won six league titles in all, which put them equal with Bath and just one behind Leicester, confirming their position as one of the best clubs in the country.

While I was losing the captaincy with England, and winning the title with Wasps, my home life was going through changes as another male entered the house with the arrival of my son, Harrison. After Kate's relatively easy experience of giving birth to Megan, it turned out to be a very different experience when Harry came along. For a start, Kate was ill the whole way through her pregnancy. She was sick and her blood pressure rose and she was in pain.

It turned out that she had something called pre-eclampsia so she was taken in for an induction. I went with her, and nothing happened at first, then it suddenly started ... she was in a lot of pain, 8cm dilated, and I thought that finally it was going to happen. But just as I'd started to relax and think that the baby was coming, the midwife shouted out for a doctor because she was worried about the monitor. Every time Kate had a contraction the baby's heart rate dropped. They said they were worried that the umbilical cord might be wrapped around his neck. Kate was oblivious to all this. Meanwhile I was panicking enough for the two of us, while looking like a complete fool in what should have been a loose-fitting surgeon's outfit but was skin-tight on me, and with the trousers coming up to my calves. I looked a right idiot.

I was with Kate throughout the birth, and I didn't want to lose eye contact with her all the way through in case she was worried. I remember going to the incubator to have a look at the baby when he was having his checks and thinking, *That's my boy*. I felt so lucky to have two healthy children, one of each sex.

Before long it was clear how different the children were from one another. Megan's very girlish, she likes colouring things in, whereas Harry, as soon as he could move, showed a preference for just knocking everything over and breaking everything. And he's a Hoover – he eats everything. I have no idea where he gets that from.

CHAPTER TWENTY-TWO:

LIONS IN SOUTH AFRICA

We all sat in the cafeteria at Wasps and put the television on. There was a good atmosphere in the room, all of us joking and chatting and taking the mickey out of each other, as we always do. Then the rugby coverage started and we all fell silent. We watched as the squad for the 2009 Lions tour to South Africa was announced. There were so many people in the room who might be picked to tour, so it was quite a tense morning, with all of us glued to the television as the selections were revealed in each position, waiting to see whether our team-mates had made it onto the plane.

They tend to announce teams with the backs first, starting with No. 15, so it's a long time before they get to the props at the end. Obviously I hoped I'd go on the tour, having missed the last Lions tour through injury, but, equally, I realised it was a miracle that I was up and playing again after all the injuries I'd had, so I had to be grateful to be at least in contention for a place. You never know whether you'll be picked to tour because it's not just about how you've been playing in the run-up to selection. On Lions tours it is not just about sending the best people, they have to send the right squad. They may decide that they want someone who can cover both sides of the scrum, or they might want to keep a whole front row together from another nation, in which case, even though you may have been playing better than the prop from Scotland, he might well get the nod because he has played with the other two guys chosen in the front row and that unit can be relied upon to play well.

The truth is that you don't have a bloody clue what they're thinking about. You might have been a great scrummager all season, but they've been looking out for a prop who is particularly good in the loose. Like all things in rugby, you just have to do your best, play the best rugby you can and be the best person you can – in other words, be a good team player as well as a stand-out individual – and hope that the selectors want you in their squad.

Having said all that very honourable stuff, the Lions tour is undoubtedly the ultimate for any rugby player, so I was desperate to get picked. As they went through the squad that would tour over the summer, we commiserated with those who hadn't been selected, and jeered and thumped those who had. Then they came to the forwards. I tried to act nonchalantly, smiling and looking round the room as if I hadn't noticed that they were about to announce whether I would be going on my second Lions tour. 'Phil Vickery,' said the presenter, as a dozen bread rolls rained down on me from everywhere, accompanied by jeers, boos and friendly slaps on the

back. It was a great moment, but one that I didn't celebrate right then because I knew that all around me there
were players who had dearly hoped that they would be
going on the Lions tour but now realised that their dream
was over. I just smiled, threw a few of the bread rolls
back, and felt this warm glow inside. I remember my Mum
calling, soon after my name had come up on Sky, and she
was really excited, squealing and shouting on the other
end of the phone, while I had to appear calm and relaxed
about it in front of the other guys. Inside, I was screaming
and shouting just as much as she was.

Lions tours are special. I'm the most patriotic guy in the
world, and when I am wearing the England shirt, and
singing the national anthem, I feel like I own the world,
but the Lions tour is something special on a different
level – it's right up there on its own. Is there any other
sport in the world in which Lions tours would still happen?
Despite the sport going professional, and all the commitments that players have now to their clubs and to the
national team, it's brilliant that Lions tours keep going. I
remember watching the Lions when I was a little boy. I
saw the 1989 tour to Australia. I don't remember much
about the tour except for the fact that Mike Teague had
someone by the neck (this maybe says more about me
than about Lions tours). There were some great players
in that Lions team like Finlay Calder, David Sole, Dai
Young, Jerry Guscott, Rob Andrew and Gavin Hastings.
Teague was the man of the tour, I remember that.

As well as watching Lions tours when I was young, and
being lucky enough to go on tour to Australia in 2001, I
understood something about the history of the Lions.

Obviously I knew about Willie John McBride and what his team managed to achieve. I knew about the heritage and history that goes with the Lions tour, and that's what makes it so magical. I love the fact that supporters, as well as players, can drop their national allegiances for a summer, and become Lions fans – the Scots cheering the Welsh players, the Irish cheering the English players, the Welsh cheering the Irish players. It's all just brilliant. The way the supporters get on with one another is a real credit to the sport all year round, and on Lions tours you realise just what a pleasure it is to be involved in this sport. It's a uniquely rugby thing and I applaud it and was bloody chuffed to death to be selected to travel to South Africa, even if I couldn't show that when we were sitting in the Wasps cafeteria.

Lions tours strip everyone back. No matter how experienced you are, how famous, rich or well regarded as a player, you have to drop all when you arrive on a Lions tour and you're in the same boat as everyone else, playing with people you've never played with before, rooming with people you hardly know, and having to build bonds and relationships with a whole load of new people. It's not like when you first start playing for England, and you turn up and everybody else knows one another, knows the hotel, knows the training drills and understands what is expected, and you are the odd one out. On Lions tours, to a man you turn up there not quite sure what it's going to be like. You don't know what the coaches will be like to work with, what the other guys in the front row will be like, and how the tour will progress off the field as well as on it. You just don't have a bloody clue what's going to happen, and that's one of the great delights of playing for the Lions.

One of the things I learnt from playing under Clive Woodward was how much difference one bad egg can make to a team. Clive used to talk to us about energy givers and energy sappers. He wanted a team full of people who inspired other people, and were full of energy. He didn't want anyone in the team, or even on the fringes of the team, who was anything less than upbeat and positive because of the impact they would have on other players. He called people like this energy sappers, and made an effort to eliminate them from the team.

One thing I noticed straight away about the 2009 touring side was that everyone was upbeat. We all got on very well and everyone made the effort to mix and to chat. Ian McGeechan, our head coach for that Lions series, is like Clive in that he doesn't tolerate energy sappers, and always has good men in his team. That was certainly the case on that tour. You only need one bad egg and it can disrupt all the team dynamics and make it hard for everyone else. I'm pleased to say there was no one like this on the Lions tour; everyone was there for the good of the team. Of course, every single one of us wanted to be in the Test team and do ourselves proud in the Lions shirt, and that's the way it should be, but it was more than that. Everyone was training hard and encouraging each other as well as worrying about getting into the team.

I was so pleased to be selected for the Lions because when I moved from Gloucester to Wasps many people thought I was dead and buried, clinging on to a career that had long passed. To come back and get a Lions cap after that was amazing.

Not that I ever thought the tour would be one long party or a succession of easy victories. South Africa is the hardest place to go and play rugby – it's the ultimate test of you as a player. And I knew that the Test matches in particular would be very hard, keenly fought and even brutal at times.

The tour started very glamorously with a party at the National History Museum to send us on our way. We had photographs taken with us standing next to the dinosaurs. If you can't enjoy that, you can't enjoy anything. I sat there looking around, thinking, *I'm with some of the greatest players in the world here and we're in this fabulous museum being photographed by photographers from around the world.*

You have to be able to enjoy these benefits and realise how bloody lucky you are to be playing in this great team, alongside great players, and in the footsteps of some of the best players ever to wear a rugby shirt. Twelve years ago, when the Lions were last in South Africa and won the Test series, I was a young player making my way in the game. I watched bits and pieces of it on television without fully understanding the enormity of it, but like most young props I'd been an ardent supporter of Oz du Randt, the awesome Springbok loosehead, since seeing him play in the World Cup a couple of years earlier. Then, in 2007, I played against him in the World Cup final and lost. Disappointed as I was, I still felt happy for him – proud for him, in fact – when he picked up his winner's medal that night in Paris. And when I saw him afterwards I gave him a big hug. It just goes to show what a silly old sentimental sod I am. I was looking forward to meeting up with him again.

We flew to South Africa and I was teamed with Jamie Heaslip, the Irish No. 8, to start with, but we changed rooms all the time as we moved around the country, so that we got the chance to room with quite a few other players, and get to know them well. With England, we were used to having our own rooms, and I know Clive had fought hard for us to have single rooms when training or competing for England, but the Lions is different. You arrive out there without knowing many of the other players very well, but have to get to know them well very quickly to have a chance of bonding properly as a team so that you can effectively compete against one of the best teams in the world.

Over the course of the tour I shared a room with Ronan O'Gara and Luke Fitzgerald, among others. To be honest I wasn't at all bothered who I shared a room with. I think everyone else is the same. You just get on with the person you're sharing with and get to know them a bit better. On the tour we were travelling a great deal and playing two games a week, so we were on the go the whole time and living out of suitcases. It meant a lot of changing places, hotels and room-mates. Whoever had to sit down and make a plan for who should room with whom at each stage of the tour, to make sure that all the different nationalities and all the different positions got to mix properly throughout the course of the tour, should have received some sort of medal! It was great fun when we were travelling around in these distinctive great big red buses with the Lions logo down the side. Just seeing those buses made me feel proud, realising that I would once again be fulfilling the dreams of so many people back at home.

When we first arrived we did a fair amount of meeting and greeting – meeting kids in schools and the town-ships, attending official functions, going to welcoming parties, garden parties, barbecues and golf days. A lot of these events were good fun, but when there are so many to do, it can get to the stage where you just want to be left alone for a while.

Working with kids was great, though; there's a huge amount of poverty in South Africa which is very scary to witness. It was very emotional when you saw these chil-dren no older than my children, with nothing in the world and no family to look after them. The kids loved the rugby. Their faces lit up when we all trooped off the bus, in our Lions tracksuits, and clutching rugby balls.

When you go to South Africa, you always worry about how safe it is, and whether it's OK to go out to the shops or even wander into the grounds of the hotel. You hear all these horrible statistics about how Johannesburg is the murder capital of the world and you think, bloody hell, I best not even leave my room without a gun then. Johan-nesburg is a hell of a long way from Bude, I have to tell you ...

When we were there on Lions duty, we were well looked after. We had South African security and our own security looking after us. We had to be sensible, and go everywhere in groups, always letting the security guards know where we were going. They said if we did that, we'd be fine.

I find South Africa a frustrating country. It's a great place, but it has so many issues to deal with. You look at the Garden Route and how beautiful that is, you see the lions and other amazing creatures and plants that survive there and you think that it should be the most perfect place on earth. There's the weather, the fantastic food and drink, the coastline, the people and that mountain. Look at Table Mountain – it's one of the most spectacular sights in the world. The country has got everything. They have a huge passion for sport, magnificent hotels, I could go on and on and on ... and I find it really frustrating that they can't get the social stuff right and they can't look after their people properly. The shanty towns and signs of abject poverty everywhere are awful, and a reminder of just how much the country's been through. I hope they find a way to use the country's massive resources to help the people who have absolutely nothing.

Back on the training ground, the coaches kept things open right up until the first Test. None of us had any idea whether we would be playing in the match. We didn't know what the combinations would be – nothing. As well as none of us knowing whether we would be playing, the coaches also kept things very simple. There were no complicated set pieces or overdone training sessions to get us to understand new moves and new strategies. We were at the end of a long season, so they planned things to ensure that we didn't have to have endless exhausting sessions in the heat. It was just about fine tuning. It felt as if everything was well organised, and we all started to relax and feel as if we were in very safe hands. With Ian McGeechan as the head coach, we shouldn't have had any doubts.

As well as the normal rugby training sessions and fitness training with Craig White, the Lions fitness guy, we also did a certain amount of hypoxic training to get us into shape to play at altitude. This training was well organised and there was a lot of it, but you have to remember that for every one of the smaller teams coming up against us on tour this clash with the Lions was the biggest match of their lives and they desperately wanted to win. They would have trained for, planned for and peaked for this match all season, so you had to take them as seriously as you would any international team, and play the best rugby you could, or you risked coming badly unstuck before you even got to the Test matches.

On some Lions tours there is a real division between the Test side and the non-Test side. Geech dealt with this well by keeping the team selection for matches wide open, so that everyone felt they were in with a shout. Even with someone as fair as Geech, though – indeed on every Lions tour – there's a certain confrontation between being a team player and being an individual on the pitch. You want to stand out in those mid-week matches so that you get picked for the Test team, but equally you want to be a good team player and help everyone else look good, so that you win the matches. I think we had clever selectors on that tour who understood that players were often doing good work that wasn't always easily seen. But I know that on other tours it has been a problem.

As the tour got going, and we began moving from place to place, I started to get to know some of the other players who I hadn't previously known very well. One of the things I really enjoy about going on a Lions tour is seeing all the other players, and getting closer to them. Over the weeks you see the way they play, the way they train and their attitude, and you get to know them much better. It's interesting to see how their character comes out as the tour progresses. You find out a lot about players on a long tour like the Lions tour to South Africa. There's no hiding place when there are two matches a week, and everyone's sharing rooms.

Although the Test matches are obviously the ones that everyone wants to win, the early games can be very difficult in their own way because you're playing with a team that has not played together before, so you're all learning everything from scratch. Everyone's habits need to be learnt, you need to understand what they do under pressure, how they react when they've got a bunch of lunatics coming at them trying to rip their heads off. You learn all that in the opening games. It's special because you're bringing together all these guys and making them into a team. It's hard work. It's hard to be the very best but that's what makes it great.

The first match of the tour was against the Royal XV at altitude, and I was on the bench. The opening game on tour is about getting the rustiness out of your system. You go through the things you've been working on to see how your team-mates respond in a match situation. You realise you need to hit the line twice as fast, and that's something you take back to training sessions to get right for the next game. We won 37–25 but we hadn't played brilliantly. I don't think anyone came off the pitch feeling fully happy with his performance. But we all knew we couldn't dwell on it. When you're on tour you have to take the lessons from the match you're playing, then forget the match and move on. You have to keep looking forward, and keep concentrating on trying to enjoy it. Disappointments have to be buried on tour – you can't stop and sulk or you'll drag everyone else down too.

Match two was against the Golden Lions. We won 74–10, which was great and helped alleviate the disappointment we'd felt at the way we played in the first match. We finally got our rhythm going. Journalists started to ask who I thought would get into the Test team, but I honestly wasn't thinking about that at this stage. I was taking each match at a time or I would have got myself into real trouble by looking forward and not playing my best in the game in front of me.

I was enjoying the tour. I missed the kids, of course, but phoned home to talk to them every day. Mum and Kate weren't out there. It's hard work if you've got kids around when you're trying to play, and Kate would have been left alone with them all the time, so we thought it would be better if she stayed in Gloucester with her parents. There's no doubt that it was hard to leave them behind, and by the time I got back I found that they'd grown up so much that it quite upset me. I don't want to miss one part of their growing up, I want to see it all, but you have to make sacrifices if you're going to play international rugby.

We went on to play Free State Cheetahs who we scraped past, 26–24, and Natal Sharks who we beat 39–3.

Against Natal Sharks I got myself into a bit of bother. I clattered into rucks and mauls for the first ten minutes of the game before being shown a yellow card by Jonathan Kaplan, the referee. He told me I was 'at best reckless', but his words were nowhere near as menacing as those of Warren Gatland, who really gave it to me in the neck at training the next morning. The Lions' forwards coach tore filthy great strips off me for my indiscipline. He gave me a right rollicking. I thought I was completely in the doghouse, but then Geech came to me and asked me whether I would captain the team against Western Province.

I'll admit it was a great honour and quite a surprise considering everything that Warren said. But the great thing about the Lions coaches was that they didn't sulk or mope or moan. They said what they thought, then moved on; there was no nastiness hanging in the air at any time on the tour. People had the confidence to speak their mind.

When Geech asked me, I said 'yes' straight away and thought, *That's another one to tell the kids*. Captaining a Lions side is a big thing. It's different from captaining the national side – it's a bigger responsibility because you're representing the whole of Britain and Ireland abroad, and you don't know the players as well, so captaining is more important and thus more difficult.

It was also a big deal because we hadn't lost a match on tour so far, and I really didn't want to be captain of the first Lions side to lose on this tour. I knew that the game against Western Province was very dangerous because the first Test was round the corner and defeat could shatter confidence and undermine morale and, more importantly, it could make me look like a useless prat.

Being captain is a huge honour but it doesn't come without its difficulties and this was a tough match in which we had to work hard for every point. We won 26–23, and afterwards I was glad it had been a hard game. We needed to really push ourselves with just one match left before the Test matches started, and that was no bad thing – it gave us the chance to really test ourselves. Our final game before the first Test was against Southern Kings and we won 20–8.

We'd kept up a winning run leading up to the first game against the Springboks and we were all desperate to beat them too and show that the Lions were still a force to be reckoned with, and not an outdated institution that belonged to the amateur era. I was reminded why being a Lion is the greatest experience in rugby every day as I had my hand shaken by Welshmen, Irishmen and Scots, then a couple of days before the first Test I went downstairs in the hotel for a hot chocolate and heard a noise from the bar. 'Swing Low, Sweet Chariot' was being belted out by guys dressed in Lions shirts, and when they'd finished they sang 'Bread of Heaven'. In the time I was there, drinking my chocolate, they sang the whole songbook from the four Lions nations in succession. It was a pretty special experience to hear that, and a reminder of how great the Lions are.

A massive 15,000 Lions fans had flown into Durban for the first Test. I felt energised, determined and ready to beat South Africa, but as I finished my hot chocolate and headed up to bed I had no idea that the game would be one of the most dreadful experiences of my life.

CHAPTER TWENTY-THREE:

CRASHING DOWN

The first 2009 Lions Test. Christ, do I have to talk about this? Can we not just move on to the third Test? That was much more interesting. No? OK, I'll start at the beginning, right from the moment I woke up on that fateful day.

On the morning of the first Test I was up at around 7 a.m., still groggy from the sleeping tablet the night before. I always struggle to sleep before matches, especially Test matches, and the sleeping pills knock me out cold. When I woke up that morning I felt woozy, like the feeling you get when you're emerging from an operation and still feeling the after-effects of the anaesthetic.

The next thing I did was to get some fuel inside me – it's just about the only thing I do that could be described as a superstition. I like to make sure I take on board some good, slow-release carbohydrates at the beginning of the day, before I get caught up in all the Test match excitement, but it's become such a big psychological thing with me that if I don't have my porridge it can affect my ability to perform. When I came down to breakfast that morning, the first thing I noticed was the silence. This tends to be the case on the day of an important match. It still surprises me now that you can tell the seriousness of a match by the lack of talking that goes on over breakfast.

After eating, I went back up to my room and thought about the key things I had to remember that day. I looked down at the notes I'd made and tried to think about everything that was expected of me. I thought about what I'd cocked up in training and what I had to make sure I got right today. *What was the first move? What did I have to do when I got there?*

There's a thin line between remembering everything you need to for the match ahead, and fretting over all the expectations of you so much that you can barely function. I wanted to read through the key points I had to remember without getting myself into a blind panic about the Test.

I also visualised the match and visualised us succeeding and doing everything right. Visualisation is an important technique that I learnt through Dave Alred, one of the coaches who worked with the England players. He specialised in kicking, and was Jonny Wilkinson's kicking coach, but he was also an expert in sports psychology, and used to work with us on areas like visualisation in which you close your eyes and focus with all your might on picturing yourself performing successfully. There's a lot of evidence that if you concentrate on picturing yourself doing something right time and again you will actually increase your chances of doing it right in competition.

I didn't do too much or worry myself too much. I tried to keep calm and not get anxious because I didn't want to waste nervous energy that should be saved for the game.

Psychology has become a more and more important part of rugby, and I have found myself thinking hard about ways in which I can be better prepared, mentally, for games. I had watched how tennis players prepare to return serve and seen how they were always alert, always ready to go, then as soon as the server threw the ball up to serve, that was it – they were on their toes and in the game, ready to return serve the minute the ball came over. I noticed that whichever way the ball went, and whichever part of the service box the ball landed in, they'd be ready to return it straight away. I knew that's what I needed to be like, so I thought that morning about tennis players waiting to return serve – on their toes, alert, awake, ready.

When I was sure that I knew what the main points were for the match, I put the television on for a while and just lounged around, trying to kill time without getting stressed out. If they'd started talking about the match on television, I would have switched it off. I don't tend to watch rugby shows on television and I very rarely read newspapers. I stopped doing that a while ago because it's worthless to read that stuff. There's no point in throwing someone else's viewpoint into the equation. Even the best-informed journalist doesn't really know what's going on in the training sessions and doesn't know what we're aiming to do, so listening to them, or reading their stories and taking their views on board, would be a huge mistake.

Mid-morning we had a get-together of the team, where we walked through the lineouts and the coaches checked that everyone was OK. It was a very relaxed affair. Once they'd decided that everyone was alive and not ill or anything, the session ended, and it was time for the pre-match meal. I'm not a great fan of the pre-match meal, as long as I've had my porridge first thing. I never eat much at the meal and often, when I do, I'm sick.

For me, match-day preparation is like preparing to make a long car journey. You check the oil, the air in the tyres, the petrol, and then you know that you've done the right thing and the rest is down to luck. If you break down and you've prepared properly, at least you can say that you did all you could. I'm like that with rugby matches. If I've got myself in the best shape possible in the weeks leading up to a match and prepared for the game itself, then at least I know that I've done all I can.

My three main things that I did that morning were to check:

1. **Hydration** – had I taken enough water on board?
2. **Energy** – had I eaten my big bowl of porridge in the morning?
3. **Mental preparation** – had I run through the plays, calls and tactics in my mind before leaving for the match? Was I ready for what the game would throw at me? Was I prepared for everything? One of the key things Geech had said to us was that we had to get up quickly from rucks, no matter how much we'd been battered and bruised. He told us that when it comes down to it, it's a numbers game – the team

with more guys on their feet is going to win.
Sometimes when you're in a ruck, you can convince
yourself that you can't get up because there are
people on top of you, but you've got to. It's your job
to get up. You've got to push people off you and
force yourself onto your feet or you're no use to
anyone. I went through this in my mind and pictured
myself doing that in the match.

Once it was time to leave, we all piled onto the coach.
Again it was very quiet, with no one speaking and everyone lost in their own world. Most of the guys had iPods
on and listened to their own music all the way to the
ground. I didn't. I just sat there quietly, lost in my own
thoughts until we arrived at the stadium.

I get quite emotional on match days, and end up feeling like I'm about to burst into tears one minute, and
burst into song the next. It's the most peculiar thing. I sat
there on the coach thinking about my kids and how much
they mean to me and feeling happy and determined that
I wasn't going to let them down. Then I thought of what
a big Test match this was and became almost paralysed
with grief that I was bound to let everyone down – it was
awful. Terrible. *What was I going to do?* The next minute
I was happy again and confident that everything was
going to be fine.

We arrived at the ground around an hour and a half
before kick-off, giving us time to sort ourselves out, without being too long so that nerves set in. When I got to
the changing room I found my spot and took a flick
through the programme before getting my taping done

– my shoulders, wrists, ankles, knees and any other parts of me that the physio felt needed to be protected. I wanted to get that done straight away, and get my warm-up kit on and studs sorted so I could relax. I didn't feel the need to rush out and take in the atmosphere because I know it changes so much when the crowds come in. I decided to warm up slowly by myself, stretching out my back and doing some skipping and running around to get the blood flowing.

I had my notes with me, with key points for me to remember written down, and I stuck that up on the wall, by my peg, and glanced at it from time to time, while getting ready.

Just before we ran on I got myself into the right state of mind for the match. I know that a lot of athletes get 'into the zone' hours before a race, but I don't do this until just before we go out, because even after we've run on there's a bit of time before we play – what with the anthems and the meeting of any dignitaries or members of the Royal family who are at the match, so if I get myself too psyched up I'll be standing there while everyone's singing the national anthems, ready to go into battle. Then, when they're over, the energy will have seeped out of me … and I'll be ready to go to bed.

From the kick-off, that first Test match was played at a furious pace. Not that that's anything to be too surprised about, it's a Test match after all. You expect it to be fast, tough and keenly fought, especially in the first quarter as you are trying to get the measure of your opponents, but this one was something else. I remember seeing a few of the guys after fifteen minutes; they were absolutely hanging. There were cries of, 'Someone kick it out, please. I can't go on.' We were all in pieces.

But there's no point me talking about the pace of the game, or how nice the grass was, or what a lovely day it was, or what the backs were up to. The main story with me in that first Test, and what became the talk of the tour, was in the scrums where I was in all sorts of trouble. I'll try and explain what it felt like for me in that bloody scrum, but even today I'm not sure what was going on.

Right from the first scrum, it was all very strange. I just couldn't get down to scrummage properly. Opposite me in the Springbok front row was a guy called Tendai Mtawarira, nickname 'The Beast', and he was causing me all sorts of trouble. I'd heard of him before the first Test, of course. In fact, I'd played against him and it wasn't like he suddenly appeared from nowhere to bugger my game up. He'd been capped a year previously and was a cult figure at Natal Sharks, but he'd never been known as an aggressive scrummager. He was known as an aggressive player around the field, and his rampaging runs had won him plenty of fans – but we hadn't been particularly concerned about him in the scrum. *So why was I having so much trouble scrummaging against him?*

We went down into the scrum and Mtawarira forced himself into me. I didn't know what was going on, but I popped up and he was awarded a penalty, which is exactly what the Springboks wanted. The frustrating thing for me was that the referee, Bryce Lawrence, a New Zealander, never intervened. He allowed 'The Beast' to squat low and fire me through the roof of the scrum, something that is totally illegal. If a player is doing something illegal and getting away with it, then so be it – good luck to them. Playing the game well often means playing the referee well. Lots of things happen on a rugby field that the referee doesn't see, and if players get away with it, they get away with it. But what was odd about this situation was that it happened time after time. Whenever we went down into a scrum, I would pop up and the referee would award a penalty against me.

The first time this happened I thought it was a fluke, and I went into the next scrum determined not to let him do it, but even though what he was doing was illegal, the referee didn't pick him up for it, and as I popped South Africa got another penalty. I didn't know what to do.

Every scrum I went into felt strange. I couldn't get down properly and every time I tried to the referee would blow up and penalise me. It was awful. I take nothing away from the South Africans. They played the referee and they played the game, and they won the scrummaging, but it was very odd. The referee seemed unable or unwilling to do anything about it. Without a solid scrum, we didn't get any sort of grip on the game.

We were all appealing to the ref to sort the scrum out, but he ignored our appeals and continued to penalise us. When I bumped into the ref the week after, he took a bit of a nervous step back when I approached him, but then we talked and he told me that he had watched the tape and said he might have got some things wrong. I thought, *Well, it's a bit f—king late now!* I don't know why he didn't act at the time and realise what a mess the scrums were in.

Five minutes into the second half I was replaced and came off the field to chants of *'Beast, Beast, Beast!'* I remember one really fat guy in a South African shirt shouting *'Beast!'* at me and clapping when I went past him. Things like that don't bother me, though. I'm my own biggest critic and I know when I did well or badly.

The period after that first Test was the hardest of my career. I don't think the guys knew what to say to me afterwards. We had lost the match 26–21 and I'd been humiliated on the pitch. To be honest I didn't need to be told anything. I'd been there, right in the middle of it all. I knew just how badly it had gone. None of the coaches came up to me and said, 'You didn't do very well there.' They didn't need to.

Everyone was supportive. They kept saying that I hadn't become a bad player overnight. They told me to forget about it, put it to bed and move on. I nodded and told them that I would, but lying in bed at night I had far from forgotten about it. I tried not to feel sorry for myself but I was so mad at what happened that it was hard.

You can't mope about something like that or dwell on it after the game because you're still around the guys so you have to remain motivated and upbeat. But I felt awful, absolutely bloody awful. When you're on a Lions tour, the next match is only ever a few days away and we were due to play Emerging Springboks three days after that first test, so me wandering round like a miserable bastard wasn't going to help anyone.

I still had to get onto the coach and go into the changing room and I knew there was maybe a 1% chance that I'd be used in the next match, so I had to prepare for it. I found it tough after that game, to be honest, because it felt like everything had come crashing down. I tend to take things personally when I have a bad game, but you have to move on quickly or you'll make the whole thing so much worse for yourself and everyone else.

In the second test Adam Jones took my place. He'd come on to replace me in the first Test, and I was aware that it was most likely he would be playing the whole of the second Test, so I wasn't surprised or upset when I found I wouldn't be in the side. But then during the match he was badly injured. I was in the physio's room when he was brought off the pitch and in next to me. He was lying on a bench screaming as two blokes tried to get his arm back into the socket. It was bloody painful to watch him going through it. As a fellow front-row – and with my injuries – I understand what that's like. Gethin Jenkins came off too and had a facial fracture that was so bad he looked like the Elephant Man. I had to ring his missus to tell her that he'd got a cheek fracture and would be out of the rest of the tour. The Lions lost 28–25, we knew we had lost the tour, and had just pride to play for in the final Test. I was aware that the injury to Adam might well mean me being selected for the third Test and having the chance to put right all that had gone wrong in the first one.

People talked of it being a 'huge psychological chal-lenge' for me to overcome, and in many ways they were right. After the nightmare of Durban, I couldn't imagine getting onto the field again during the tour. It was hard as the days leading up to the third Test passed. I was the one that all the journalists wanted to talk to, and I knew everyone would be watching to see how I would cope this time.

The crowd were desperate for South Africa to clean sweep us in the series after we'd beaten them the last time the Lions toured in 1997, with Martin Johnson as captain and Geech, once again, as coach. On the previous Lions tour in 2005 the guys hadn't won a match and I think we were all aware deep down that it was important for us to win this game, to show that the Lions could still win, and there was a place for Lions tours in the rugby calendar, although my concerns were more about how the bloody hell the scrums were going to go this time, and whether the referee would let their front row get away with illegal play throughout the match as he had last time.

That first scrum was interesting. When the referee called it you could feel the tension in the air, and I could hear voices in the crowd still shouting *'Beast, Beast, Beast!'* at me. But we were prepared for anything. The Beast might do the same thing this time, and it wasn't just me coping with him trying to pop me up; we had a whole pack aware of what his tactics were, and standing rigid and determined not to let him get his way.

I also think that after all the debate in the press in the weeks before this third Test, the referee would have been more attuned to what was going on, and we might have got a more sympathetic hearing than we had in the first Test. The scrums worked fine, and we won 28–9 to end the series on a winning note at last.

From a personal point of view, I was relieved to have been given the chance to get back out there and put right what had gone wrong in the first Test. I was also very pleased that we won and was aware of how important that was for the whole future of the Lions. I had played in the last winning Lions game before the 2009 tour, and then played my part in winning this last Test. In both my Lions tour experiences I've been able to pass on a winning jersey. Things like that matter to me because the Lions matter to me, and the guys who are selected to play for the Lions matter to me a lot.

We had a few drinks that night and celebrated our win. The South Africans were very gracious about their series victory, John Smit in particular. We'd had such a good time throughout and we got to know each other and trust one another. Back at the hotel in the bar, relief and sadness were mixed. We all felt that it was close to being a victorious tour, and it was disappointing not to have been able to make it one.

I took away from the Lions tour the experience of having worked with great coaches and good guys. We built brilliant relationships off the pitch, and we fought hard on the pitch. We were a very close group and it was strange when we arrived back at Heathrow, got off the plane and went to the carousel to collect our bags and then it was all over. We went our separate ways, and would never be together as a group again. I did text a few of the players, and stayed in touch with some, and you know they're there if you need them, but pretty much everyone goes back and picks up their life that they left behind when a tour is over.

CHAPTER TWENTY-FOUR:

PAIN IN THE NECK

I returned from the Lions tour, and after a little break to spend time with Kate and the kids I got back into the swing of things at Wasps and was selected to captain the side in the Amlin Challenge Cup against Racing Metro. It was a great honour to be asked, of course, as it always is, but things didn't go as planned when I went into a scrum and it went down too quickly.

My head went down as the front rows collapsed and I came up feeling dazed and as if I'd crushed my head. It was really painful days later so I decided to get it checked out and headed once again for the offices of Rick Nelson. I explained to him that I was really struggling because my neck was in agony and both my arms were in real pain. He scanned the area and found that the disc had shunted into the spinal cord on the left-hand side. Rick told me that the condition of my neck was much worse and now it was really quite serious. There was major compression on the C7 nerve and great pressure on my spinal cord. Rick said, 'What do you want to do?' I said I wanted to play again.

He said that for me to have any chance of playing again he would have to actually remove the bulging disc to alleviate the pain. He couldn't take away any fragments; the whole thing had to come out. He made it very clear that this was a major operation and I shouldn't go into it without thinking about it seriously. The trouble was, I was in so much pain that I had to make a quick decision and all I could think was, *Just do whatever you can to get me out of pain and in a position where I can start playing rugby again soon.*

The only way in which he could remove the disc was to go through the front of my neck. The operation is known as an anterior cervical discectomy. Rick explained that when you go through the front of the neck to get to the disc you have to go through the disc to get it out or you end up doing damage all around it, so it's quite an intricate operation, and means you take out the padding in the disc.

The classic thing to do when you remove a damaged disc is to fuse the discs either side of it with a bone graft taken from another part of the body. The trouble is if you fuse one of the discs, you put more stress on the other discs. There was no alternative to this years ago, and this is the operation that Jason Leonard had when he had serious neck problems. They took a piece of bone out of Jason's pelvis and used it to fuse together two discs in his neck. The problem with this is that it does mean the rest of the neck is more vulnerable and the process can accelerate wear and tear.

Rick wanted to try and avoid doing that with me because disc replacements have been developed in the last few years – these tiny ball-and-socket joints that slip into the spine. It's not a standard thing to do for rugby players because no one knows how they will respond to the hits in rugby. Rick had previously used the technique on Steve Thompson and it appeared to have been a success, so he thought that would be the best thing for me, but he emphasised that this was a very new operation, and they really hadn't been designed with rugby players in mind. Rick said that every time he watched Steve Thompson going into contact he would be thinking about the tiny little disc in Steve's neck, and wondering how it was holding up.

So into hospital I went and Rick and his team of super-surgeons decompressed the nerve root, then carried out the disc replacement. When I came round from the operation the pain had lifted straight away. There was a different pain, from the operation, but that awful pain that I had been struggling with for days had gone. I didn't mind the new pain. Being a prop I'm kind of used to pain anyway. There are very few rugby players who are 100% fit on any day. At least this pain was the result of an operation and I knew it would get better in time. It was a massive relief.

You try to be brave when you've got an injury, and not to complain about the pain, but the way I had suffered before this operation had been worse than anything else I'd ever experienced. I couldn't sleep at night so was always tired, and was never quite with it because of the painkillers I was taking. Night starts to turn into day when you're like that, and everything becomes blurred. It was horrible.

After the operation I felt much better, but I was still not sure whether I would be able to play again. My neck would need a lot of work to make it strong enough to withstand scrum time, so I knew I wouldn't be able to shortcut the rehabilitation and get back to playing rugby very quickly.

I had to sit around at home watching while England struggled along, getting criticism from all sides, and the management being written off as useless. Martin Johnson came in for much of the blame, of course, which annoyed me. I think players need to look at themselves when things don't go right on the pitch. It can't just be about blaming coaches. I watched a lot of those England matches and thought to myself, *I don't think some of the guys are good enough.* To be an international player, you need to do more. You have to be a bit different. You have to set your standards a bit higher. You cannot, in my opinion, just be a normal club player and expect to go and compete successfully at international level. You've got to make sacrifices. It might be an extra five minutes of handling or an extra couple of hits on the tackle shield when the others have gone in.

It might be saying to your mates, 'I'm not coming out tonight.' It might be going to bed a little earlier. Silly as it may sound, all these bits and pieces add up. And it's something people must take on board, because there's lots we all can do. I'm not a believer in just pointing fingers and saying this and that is wrong. England didn't win the Six Nations, meaning that we hadn't won the title since 2003, the year in which we won the World Cup.

Away from the rugby field, I began working hard on Raging Bull, a sportswear company that I'd first had the idea for back in 2000. I wanted to have a go at using my name 'Raging Bull' and see whether it would work as a commercial brand. It was going well – selling rugby kit to clubs, universities and schools, as well as having a leisurewear division that was taking off – but I was keen to expand it. Andy Deacon was employed as the sales-man, selling into rugby clubs, and I'd managed to get the range into Debenhams, which was a great coup!

I wanted to make a success out of the company because I know as well as anyone how an injury can come along at any time and take the sport from you. You're only in rugby for a relatively short amount of time and while you're playing you want to focus every ounce of your energy on the game, but it is important, later in your career, to look ahead and consider what you are going to do next.

I hoped I might have the right genes in me to make a successful businessman because of the way my grand-parents made business successes of the farms they have run. It's very difficult to make any sort of money out of farming, and when I look back I admire the way my grandparents were able to create two businesses out of one.

I wanted to expand Raging Bull as much as possible. I developed a range of ladies' clothing called Moody Cow (I know, it's a bit naughty, but it's meant to be tongue-in-cheek) and children's clothing and wanted to think about other opportunities. I tried to use a lot of the lessons I'd learnt in rugby when thinking about the business. I thought about the way in which Clive Woodward had taken charge of the England squad in 1997. He brought a very definite business edge to the sport. I remember the way he said that it was difficult to make a 10% difference in any area of the game, but that we could make 10% differences in different areas. Could I do that with the business? Make every area of the business just that little bit better to create a real overall difference to the way the business was functioning?

I first launched Raging Bull when I noticed a gap in the market for high-quality sportswear, so I decided to do a range that was halfway between White Stuff and a performance sports brand. We had branched out by doing a deal with Mitsubishi, the car manufacturer, to create a Raging Bull vehicle which was fun. I still love it when I see a car go past with the bull logo on it. There are no limits really if you develop a strong brand with a clear identity, and I wanted to think about the ways in which I could develop Raging Bull even further.

I loved the fact that the brand was synonymous with me and my reputation as a rugby player. I also loved seeing people wearing the shirts in the street. In Italy people were walking around the airport in Raging Bull tops, which was astonishing to see. Kate said that people were wearing it on the train up to Edinburgh for one international. It makes me very, very proud of the brand. I suppose my dream is for people to wear it without even knowing that I'm behind it, just choosing it because it's good, well-made clothing.

I am not an expert on stitching or weaving but I know what goes into a line of clothing, and I've learnt a lot about the business from the people I've brought in to work alongside me. It is equally as important to understand turnaround times and lead times and the business side of things as it is to understand about the fabric, buttons and design, and I'm learning a lot, all the time. When you start looking at other brands and how they're expanding and which shops sell which concessions, you get a feel for why certain brands are successful and others aren't.

Obviously, marketing and promotions are key if the clothing is really going to take off, and I'm at the difficult point at the moment where I need to throw money into the promotion of the brand but don't want to use up all the money in the company doing that, and find myself unable to pay people and struggling to keep the company afloat.

The great thing about having Raging Bull is that I can use what I've learnt in sport to develop the business because, in my experience, a lot of skills I've learnt transfer from sport to business. It is all about performance. Success is about getting the performance right, and you look at people who've been able to do that and learn everything you can from them.

I've got lots of great people involved in helping me with Raging Bull. Actually, a funny thing happened with two of them – Richard and Fiona York – whose son did a bike ride through India and he stopped off while he was there to meet people and get to know some of the locals. He met a rugby development officer and gave the guy some of our kit (we're very keen, at Raging Bull, to help out by giving kit to communities that struggle to afford it, and to generally help out in the rugby world, and support grassroots sides). The development officer mentioned this kid called Sailen Tudu, who was a real star. They went to have a look at Sailen play, and he was scoring tries on wasteland in Calcutta. He was naturally talented, a really gifted player.

We had contacts at Hartpury College in Gloucester where we knew the principal, Malcolm Wharton, and we spoke to him about giving this kid a trial. The whole thing worked out brilliantly and Sailen got in and was given a scholarship. He's gone from living in a mud hut with no water or electricity to having a £40,000 scholarship. The guy is 20 years old now and he didn't touch a rugby ball until five years ago. Since we spotted him he's been capped by India and is tipped for a professional career. It was great that happened and I'm thrilled to have played a small part in it.

Raging Bull has been a fun company to be involved with. It's important to me that life's fun. One of my philosophies is not to take things too seriously. I think some people start doing things for all the right reasons – because they enjoy them – then lose sight of that as time goes on, and they start to take it all very seriously. I think you need to try hard never to lose sight of the reason why you started doing something in the first place. I started rugby because I enjoyed the fun and friendships of the sport. After over ten years in the game it would be easy to forget that. Yes, when you're an England player it feels serious sometimes, and when you're scrumming down against a bloke called The Beast and he's got you popping up all over the place, it's more serious than it ever was down in Bude, but it's still got to be fun. It's still got to be enjoyable, and you've got to love doing it.

There's no doubt that rugby has become a tougher game to play as I've got older. My mobility has decreased thanks to age and the many operations I've had, but you just learn to adapt. We talk at Wasps all the time about how to be technically good so you don't have to use up so much energy. When he was coaching England, Andy Robinson used to talk a lot about arriving at the breakdown having made a decision. You don't want to arrive and then work out *what to do*; you want to go in knowing what you're *going to do*. You can be much more effective that way. If you know what's going to happen when you get to the breakdown, then you can choose the right line from the start. You can work out what is needed and play intelligent rugby. When you're older, it's vital that you do this. I enjoy that side of things ... thinking through the strategy and planning of games.

Having said that, I'm not sure whether I will go into coaching after playing, but I do hope to stay in the game. One thing that interests me a great deal is working with players to help them with their careers and their futures after rugby. Because rugby went professional relatively recently, there are lots of people in the game advising players who never played the game professionally themselves and simply don't understand how hugely different the sport is today from when they were players. I went through the transition and I know very well how vastly different it all is now, and how that affects the players. Having coped and succeeded as an elite professional player, I think I'd like to give back to the sport by offering advice to youngsters – almost warning them of the pitfalls of the professional game – because I think the one thing that is never addressed is the perils of fame and money. I know that sounds stupid, and given the choice everyone would like to be paid for doing what they love to do, but there is a dark side to becoming well known, as well as a pleasant side. It's nothing sinister but I think we should warn young rugby players that life will change if you become famous.

You just have to have your eyes open and be aware; you just need to be careful that you don't get used. You become very hard, to be honest. People have to earn your trust and respect.

I know I sound like an old git but the other message I'd give to kids starting out as professionals today is to understand how vital it is that they put some money away. I'm sure that rugby careers are going to get shorter and shorter as the sport becomes tougher and tougher. Yes, you do make a decent living while you're playing, but you might have sacrificed your education, and you'll certainly have sacrificed your start on the career ladder by opting to play rugby professionally. A rugby career doesn't last long. While other people are landing them- selves well-paid positions, you've been playing rugby, but playing rugby at a high level doesn't train you for anything. So you need to put money away while you're earning it, or you really will find yourself in trouble when you retire.

I think that to be successful in rugby you need to be a good person as well as a good rugby player. That might sound odd, but there's so much about the sport that's not about you on a field being cheered by tens of thousands of people. It's a team sport, and if you're a good team player, and popular in the team, then you'll get on much better in life. When you're injured or not picked, you are told to sit on a bench and support the guy who is wearing the shirt that you want, and you need to do it with good grace and great enthusiasm. You need to continue hoping that the team will win, even though you definitely want the shirt and you know that if the guy wearing it cocks up, the chances of you getting it are greatly improved. Still, you have to put the team first and hope he does well and that the team triumphs. That's what it takes to be a good rugby player.

Rugby is also about being able to take criticism, and it's about how you deal with the advice you're offered. Success in rugby is not always about the glory and the headlines; the really great players cope well with defeat and improve from defeat, and stay positive and team-focused. You need to learn daily and improve all the time and you'll only do that by listening to people.

One final thing I'd like to say in my Phil Vickery lecture about rugby is that you have to be doing the sport for the right reasons. If you want to become a professional rugby player in order to earn lots of money, get your name in the papers, meet the sponsors and become famous and all that, it won't work. It'll mean you losing your spirit. If you love what you do you'll be good at it, but you need to love it for what it is, and not for all the fame and money that it can bring you.

To be a great rugby player you need to be yourself. You need to trust yourself and back yourself, but you must do all this while remembering that you are part of a team. That may be the hardest part of rugby – that balance between what's best for the individual and what's best for the team. Unless you put the team first, no coach in his right mind will pick you and you'll never get the chance to be seen as a great individual.

Having said that, being a great individual is good too (I know, it's a bloody complicated business) and you need to excel in as many areas of the game as you can, and you need to be yourself. If that sounds confusing, what I mean is – don't try to be the next Jeff Probyn or Jason Leonard. Be the best version of yourself that you can be.

I love playing prop. I know that when you look at the props from other positions on the field you might think it's an absurd thing to do to yourself. The scrums leave you looking like Shrek, and you're always face down in the dirt, and the last to get up from rucks and mauls – but it's a great position to play because you are right out there, and have nowhere to hide. It buggers your back, your neck, your legs and your shoulders, and it does nothing for your looks, but it's worth it, worth every moment of pain for the joy of being right in the middle of it all, at the centre of the confrontation and at the heart of the game.

When you're playing prop it's like you're playing a completely different game – mentally and physically – to other players on the pitch. We have to get into a completely different mental state to go out there and do our job. You don't just psych yourself up for the match, you psych yourself up for every little confrontation within the match. When every scrum goes down I have to prepare myself mentally and get ready for the conflict.

The way I prepare myself is to bring out the emotion in the game. I think about my family and my wife and all the support they've given me ... when I think about the people who've supported me in my career, I feel I want to do well for them as well as myself. I think about my kids and how much they mean to me, I think about the people I've known through the years – my old PE teacher who got me started originally, the guys down at Bude who made it all so much fun when I first arrived at the club that I wanted to carry. Then I think about the guys at Redruth who made such an effort to get me down to the club and look after me as I developed my rugby skills. There are certainly people, throughout your career, who help you become the person you are.

Then you think about the guys on the field next to you, and how much you trust them and want to play well for them. You go through so much with your team-mates on tours, in training and in brutal matches, that there are friendships forged for life. Whatever position you're playing on a rugby field, you know that you can't win the match on your own. Every position on the field is different, and everyone needs to give their all in order for the team to win. When you know you could not do something were it not for your mate, he becomes that much more special. You need other people on a rugby field. You need people who will be there for you and will put in the extra inch, the extra effort, and you know how much they're hurting but still going. In the changing room beforehand everyone's relying on everyone else, and that's great, that's teamwork, and that's rugby.

In my career I've had a go at playing back row, second row and prop. The fatter I've become, the further forward I've moved. If I'm honest, I think I'd have liked to have played at No. 6. You've got a bit of grind and scrapping there that I really like, there's all the kicking and fighting that's part and parcel of rugby, but there's also some freedom to play as well. Not that I'm complaining – I love everything about rugby. I hope I'm involved in the game, in some way or other, for the rest of my days. I just can't imagine life without it.

CHAPTER TWENTY-FIVE:

MY TEAM

Christ, this is a hard thing to do. I've played with some great players in my career, and met some great characters, and I've seen some brilliant players on television that I wish I'd been able to play with. How the hell am I supposed to go through them all and choose the ones that I think are best? I remember watching rugby as a child and seeing some rugby skills that had me spellbound. But which of those players do I think should go into a fantasy XV ahead of the great players I've played with and against? It's a tough call, and I've had to miss players out who I think are world-class. I've ended up putting ten guys on the bench because I didn't want to leave anyone behind. There are 100 more I'd like to put on there but I thought it would just get a bit silly if I did that, so I made myself stop at ten!

After much thinking, worrying and chopping and changing, I have selected my all-time world XV. Now all I need to do is call these guys, tell them they've been selected, book the buses and get them out on tour.

Gareth Edwards at his prime and Jonah Lomu at his prime in the same team ... can you imagine? If only we could mess with time and throw these players together. Imagine Zinzan Brooke at No. 8 and Gareth Edwards at scrum-half ... it's pure fantasy, but lovely to think about. And if there are any problems and we need to bring on replacements, we've got J. P. R. Williams, Phil Bennett and Jonny Wilkinson on the bench, so there are no weak links. We're going to allow smoking on the bench so that Serge Blanco feels at home, and we'll allow drinking on the pitch so Jason Leonard doesn't get thirsty, and they can all have the skin-tight shirts, smart hotels and fancy travel arrangements because Clive Woodward's in the coaching squad to make sure that all happens. It's hard to see how this team can fail. I'm off to find worthy opposition ...

PHIL VICKERY'S ALL-TIME WORLD XV

(Note: teamsheets will be presented with the props first; none of this announcing the props right at the end after all the poncey backs.)

1. **Jason Leonard** (England)
2. **Sean Fitzpatrick** (New Zealand)
3. **Olo Brown** (New Zealand)
4. **Martin Johnson** (England, capt.)
5. **Ian Jones** (New Zealand)
6. **Richard Hill** (England)
7. **Finlay Calder** (Scotland)
8. **Zinzan Brooke** (New Zealand)
9. **Gareth Edwards** (Wales)

10. Michael Lynagh (Australia)
11. Jonah Lomu (New Zealand)
12. Tim Horan (Australia)
13. Jeremy Guscott (England)
14. Jeff Wilson (New Zealand)
15. Jason Robinson (England)

Replacements: David Sole (Scotland), **Graham Dawe** (England, bench capt.), **John Eales** (Australia), **Lawrence Dallaglio** (England), **Josh Kronfeld** (New Zealand), **Serge Blanco** (France), **Phil Bennett** (Wales), **Jonny Wilkinson** (England), **J. P. R. Williams** (Wales), **Philippe Saint-André** (France)

COACHING STAFF
Executive Performance Director: Sir Clive Woodward
Tour Manager: Gerald Davies
Head Coach: Sir Ian McGeechan
Backs Coach: Brian Ashton
Forwards Coach: Warren Gatland
Defence Coach: Shaun Edwards
Executive Problem Solver & Fixer: Louise Ramsay

MEDICAL TEAM
Doctor: Dr Terry Crystal
Physiotherapists: Barney Kenny and Prav Mathema

WHY THESE PLAYERS WERE CHOSEN
Jason Leonard – Jason would earn selection for his drinking skills alone. He's one of the best drinkers I've ever met in my life. His capacity for beer is the stuff of

legend and I'm proud to have shared the odd pint or two with him over the years. I'm also proud to have played alongside him in the front row because he's the best loosehead prop in the world. He'd be first on the team-sheet in my fantasy XV any day.

Sean Fitzpatrick – Fitzy is a legend. I remember growing up, watching him and thinking what a brilliant player he was. He inspired me to play to the best of my ability. His sheer competitiveness and his all-round skills on the pitch are outstanding.

Olo Brown – He's a rock. The guy doesn't move when you're scrummaging against him. He uses his weight at the scrum and you can't shift him. No matter how much you push, he goes nowhere. Never plays fancy rugby, never over-complicates things – he's just a big solid lump, and you need those in the front row.

The front row as a unit – You've got a good combination here. Fitzy can chat away to the scrum-half and sort things out while the two guys either side of him win every scrum going. To be honest, Fitzy could have a bit of a holiday with these two guys. He wouldn't have to do a thing. He could take a book, or stand out with the backs. Olo and Jase would have the scrum sorted on their own.

Martin Johnson – He's a worker. Big, strong bloke, big lips, big forehead, mono-brow ... he's got it all. He never gives up, leads by example. Few people in the world would risk missing him out of their all-time world XV.

Ian Jones – Ian would work well with Johno because he's competitive and very wiry. He's the sort of guy who never looks good in the gym and when the fitness results come in, but he knows exactly how to use his body on a rugby field. With these two in the second row the scrum won't go anywhere and the lineouts will all be won. All we need now are three belters in the back row and that's the scrum all tied up.

Richard Hill – The guy is phenomenal. For years he worked hard in the England team but was slightly under the radar, with no one but the players on the pitch aware of quite how much work he was doing. People soon realised, though, and Richard was recognised for what he is – one of the best back-row players the world has ever seen. He's never fancy, always solid, and a great guy to have in your team.

Finlay Calder – I remember watching Finlay when I was a young boy and thinking how great he was. He was always up and at it, always forcing himself on everything. In some ways he reminds me of Peter Winterbottom with that dogged determination to succeed at all costs.

Zinzan Brooke – No pack would be complete without the silky skills of Zinzan at No. 8. He broke the mould for back-row players ... running, passing and off-loading the ball, it was like New Zealand had an extra back on the pitch. He was a tough, relentless, competitive back-row player who could also kick, score tries and do all that other fancy stuff that the backs get up to. He ground out the hard yards, winning tough ball, then could actually do something with it. An amazing player.

The back row as a unit – I think this back row would have everything. I'd love to see them playing together. Actually, what I'd really love is to play prop at the front of a scrum with these three in the back row. Every ball you secured you'd know would be put to good use.

Gareth Edwards – It's hard to pick a team without this guy in, such was his impact on rugby in the 1970s. When you watch the tapes of him now, you see a player who was made to play scrum-half. He has such a great understanding of the game and of the play unfolding before him. He backed himself to go for daring runs but at the same time he worked well with the forwards and was a great link between the forwards and backs. It's very hard, obviously, to compare him with the players of today because the game's so fast, so much has changed, but when you look at Gareth in his time, and what he achieved, he set the benchmark higher than anyone else. When you watch the way he played – his vision, and his confidence to go for moves that seemed barely possible – it was amazing. Gaps opened up and Gareth went through. An exceptional player.

Michael Lynagh – It's hard to pick a player at fly-half, and I've worked with one of the world's best so it was tempting to pick him, but I've gone for Lynagh because he made the game look easy. He was steady and thoughtful. A bit of a speed bump in defence, but he linked well, talked well about the game and made things simple and straightforward. He reminds me a little of Mike Catt. I'd love to play with someone like Lynagh at No. 10. He's a leader on the pitch so could be in charge of the backs, while Johno looks after the forwards.

Jonah Lomu – I was at that time in my life starting to watch rugby properly and appreciate the skills of the world's leading players when Jonah Lomu burst onto the scene ... and the guy really did burst onto the scene. I don't think anyone has made an impact on rugby in quite the same way as Jonah did. I watched him in the 1995 World Cup, particularly the way in which he played against England in the semi-final, and realised that here was a player who was totally different to any other player before him. He rocked the game and took it worldwide, just as it was going professional, and he became a superstar.

Jeff Wilson – I've chosen another New Zealander on the other wing, which is strange really because you tend to think of great forwards when you think of New Zealand, but they've also given the world some of the best backs, and Jeff gets the nod for this team because his determination is second to none. He's different in stature to Jonah, of course, but he's a great goal-kicker and a very gifted athlete. These two would be a great combination. You'd have the best of both worlds with them in your team.

Tim Horan – He's a phenomenal player to watch. His ball carrying is great and his footwork outstanding. I thought about putting Jason Little with him, but I couldn't select two Australians in the centre; I'd never forgive myself. Actually, on the subject of Horan, it's worth mentioning here Dom Waldouck, a Wasps player who really reminds me of Horan. When you play with someone week in, week out, you learn about them, and Waldouck is going to be a huge player in the future. He can create something out of nothing. Look out for him.

Jeremy Guscott – I've put Jerry with Tim Horan because I think they make a perfect centre partnership. I played a lot with Jerry and, to be honest, people had warned me about him and told me that he could be a bit difficult. I was worried about whether we'd get on – him being from Bath and me from Gloucester, and all the rivalry between the two clubs. I have to say, though, I played with him, liked him and never had any trouble with him at all. I found him good company and he's a great player.

Jason Robinson – The final member of my team is someone I've played with a lot. I rate him so highly that I'd say that with a few more skills he could have been a prop forward! He's a very gifted player, one of the few players who, when he gets the ball, wherever he is on the pitch, you think, 'Something could be on here, something's going to happen.' He'd hang round the big guys on the pitch when we were playing, so we'd look after him (he wasn't stupid). He's as brave as brave can be and would never let you down through effort. Always good fun and always hard working, he's a good guy to be around. When I think of Jason, I think of him in the first Lions Test in 2001 scoring a try. The whole place stopped when he got the ball. There was this incredible silence for a heart-beat as everyone waited to see what would happen. I used to watch him when he was a rugby league player as well. I like league, and I support Wigan, so I was a fan long before he came over to union. I feel privileged to have played with him. He's magical.

REPLACEMENTS

David Sole – He epitomised everything that a prop should be. Always on top of everything. Always giving 110%. I remember people saying he wasn't big enough, but it doesn't matter how big you are. One of my pet hates is when players are told they're too small. If any children reading this are ever told they're too small to play rugby, think of Neil Back and David Sole – both of them 'too small' to play rugby at any level, both of them among the world's greatest rugby players. I'd love to have played with David Sole. I met him once and it was quite a big deal for me. I went over and shook his hand. It was a great moment.

Graham Dawe (Bench capt.) – Graham is selected for two principal reasons ... because he's a Cornishman, and because he's the world's most experienced bench player, ever. If anyone knows how to sit on a bench, Graham does. In all seriousness, I've chosen Graham because of his never-say-die attitude – because he ended up with five caps after eight years playing for England, with the rest of the time spent on the bench. Brian Moore was hooker at the time, which explains why Dawesy wasn't first choice, but for him to have spent so much time on the bench reminds us of just how much rugby has changed. The bench is very much part of the team today. If you're a replacement, you'll expect to come on for any one of a number of reasons: tactically, to perform a specific function because they want to rest a player, or because of the opposition's specific skills. It's not just because the player on the pitch is injured. When Dawesy was playing, the bench was rarely used because players could only be brought on if the guy on the field was too injured to continue. Poor Dawesy sat there match after match when Brian Moore hobbled round the pitch, blood pouring out of his mouth but still carrying on. It must have been a very difficult time not to be the first-choice player in a team but you never heard Dawesy complaining, he never moaned, he turned up match after match and sat there, just in case he was needed. All that experience will be put to good use in the team.

John Eales – It seems strange to put Eales on the bench since there's no doubt that he's one of the best players in the world, but he'll be a great guy to have around if anything happens to Johno, because he can replace him as world-class lock and World Cup winning captain. Eales's record speaks for itself ... what he did for Australian rugby was astonishing. Great in the lineout, and he can kick. A rugby superstar.

Lawrence Dallaglio – I had to pull Lawrence into the team. We couldn't go on tour without Lawrence. He's a player who broke the mould … he scored tries, had the pace of a wing three-quarter, the physique of a man mountain and the all-round presence in a team that would always stand out. He's a hard bastard too. People sometimes forget that about Lawrence, but he's hard as nails – he would get kicked and kicked in a match and just stand up and carry on without complaining, smiling at the guys who'd kicked him. He's a good bloke to have in the team.

Josh Kronfeld – Josh was one of the new breed of players who changed the openside position. He goes everywhere on the pitch and does everything. Always the first name on the All Blacks teamsheet. He's phenomenal. I'd love to have played with him.

Serge Blanco – Fifty fags a day but he still covered the field and was all over the game every time he played. An old-time French player who epitomised the free-running style of the French more than anyone else. I love the fact that he'd be smoking his fags in the changing room, on the bench and in the stands. There was something so real and human about him off the pitch, but so superhuman on the pitch.

Phil Bennett – He played in the same era as Gareth and they were both very gifted players. When you watch the tape of him, he could do things that other players couldn't get near to doing. They seemed to have such passion, style and skill and they were so patriotic. I was at a dinner with him recently and he was such a nice fella, a really decent bloke – the sort of guy that I'd like to take on tour.

Philippe Saint-André – Philippe has this extraordinary passion for the game and he loves props and enjoys working with front-row players. He was the ultimate finisher who knew how to score tries. He's someone I was lucky enough to play with and would definitely take him on tour with me.

COACHING STAFF
Executive Performance Director:
Sir Clive Woodward – I've chosen Clive because of the way in which he changed the game in England and, most significantly, how he changed the mindset of the players and showed us how to become winners. He set the standard for professional rugby players, and the world followed. He set the standards that everyone else aspired to. He wanted the best for you and was brilliant at getting the best out of you.

Tour Manager:
Gerald Davies – Gerald is tour manager for his wisdom and how he conducts himself. I love his way of thinking about the game, and my tour party would learn all about his experiences of playing with the greatest players ever. I'd love him to be guiding the team. When I toured with the Lions with him as manager, I learnt a great deal, I enjoyed spending time with him and found him a

complete inspiration. He conducted himself with humility and generosity.

Head Coach:

Sir Ian McGeechan – I love his company and hearing his thoughts on the game. He's bright and he brings people together. He explains things clearly and simply, and is a great ambassador for the game. He's good fun to be on tour with, but he knows when to take things seriously. On the Lions tour I was almost bored to death by some of his speeches but still I listened, because it's Geech and he knows what he's talking about. His passion for the game lifts you and leaves you on a real high.

Backs Coach:

Brian Ashton – Brian is one of the best coaches I've ever worked with. It didn't matter who you were, or where you'd come from, he made things simple and straightforward. His style of play was with no inhibitions; he freed you to be the best you could without constraints or limitations. Working with Brian gives you so much confidence in yourself and your abilities. He's a selfless coach, always worrying about the players and what he can do for them. As a prop, he was still interested in me, and in developing my game. He encouraged me to think about my running lines and think about why I was running to a certain place or in a certain way. He has a great enthusiasm for the game and it was always good fun playing with Brian. One thirty-minute attack session with Brian would wear you out but it was always fun, always a pleasure, and that's how he got the best out of you.

Forwards Coach:
Warren Gatland – I had heard a lot about Warren as a coach but hadn't worked with him until the Lions and I found out that all the good things that everyone had been saying about him were true. I loved the simplicity of him. Too many coaches over-coach and over-analyse in an effort to cover their own backs; it takes a confident coach to give the players a bit of information, then to let them get out there and get on with playing. Warren did that; he was great. I enjoyed working with him. Warren likes a drink too, which is good – he knows when to switch off, relax and be one of the boys. He understands that we're not just players but people too, and you can talk to him properly and get a good perspective on life.

Defence Coach:
Shaun Edwards – Shaun is in because he's slightly nuts and I think that's a good trait in a coach! You don't want your coaches to be too normal, down-to-earth and sane. I also love his will to win, his passion and his love of the game. He has people's respect, and that's important if you're a coach. He also has this ability to coach you as the player you are, without trying to change you. He recognises that you wouldn't be at this level if you weren't a good player, so he's not trying to change everything about you, just to help you become better and understand what the team is doing on the pitch and what your role in that is. He's more than a coach, he's become a friend and I'd pick up the phone and call him if I needed something. I hope he'd do the same.

Executive Problem Solver & Fixer:
Louise Ramsay – Louise was the organiser and fixer for England when Clive was coach and she's selected to help out with my team because she's the world's most organised person. Whatever you need, you know that if Louise can't do it, it can't be done. She works so hard and it's great to know, as a player, that you're never being fobbed off. You'd know for sure that Louise had done everything humanly possible to help you all the time. She's a good girl and has all the skills in life that I don't have, so I'm definitely taking her on tour.

MEDICAL TEAM
Doctor:
Dr Terry Crystal – Never mind being a doctor, he's great fun and a great entertainer. His sing-songs on the England coach were the stuff of legend and he has a great sense of humour.

Physiotherapists:
Barney Kenny and Prav Mathema – Barney is the world's most boring bloke but has a great understanding of the front five. He's honest and he works hard. He does the best for you and you'd trust him completely. Prav is the Wasps physio and, in my opinion, he's the best physio in the world. He treats you as a person, so when he's working on me he's not just working on 'a body', he's taking into account my age, how long I've been playing and all the injuries I've had. His treatment is very open-minded. He's a good fella.

INDEX